THE STORY OF ANGELS AND NATURE

The Story of Angels and Nature

CHRISTOPHER PAUL CARTER

Dwelling Place Ministries

Library of Congress Cataloging-in-Publication Data
Carter, Christopher Paul
The Story of Angels and Nature / by Christopher Paul Carter;
1st ed.

Summary: The history and future of our relationship with angels and nature.
ISBN 979-8-218-06435-8
[1. Angels / Christianity. 2. Religious / Christian. 3. Philosophy and Religion.]

Manufactured in the United States of America

10 9 8 7 6 5 4 3 2 1

For Melissa

Your love of Nature and the One who made it is contagious.

TABLE OF CONTENTS

Part 3: Stories of Freedom

Dear Reader,

As with any big subject, you just can't fit in all the background information you'd like. For instance, I'd love for everyone reading this book to have already read all of my previous books, as there's a reason this book is being written now, instead of 10 years ago. The information herein took that long to percolate and is built on the experiences and ponderings of the previous years.

If you've read those earlier books, great. If you haven't, don't worry. I'm going to do my best to include some qualifying background information wherever I can, even if it's nowhere near what I wish I could. In the meantime, here's the short list of assumptions I'm making about anyone who might have picked up this book by accident.

First, given the title of the book, I'm assuming you have an interest in *Nature.* Right off the bat, I'll tell you I'm going to use the words "Nature" and "Creation" interchangeably. I'll even capitalize them both just like the words "Universe" or "Cosmos." Think of these terms as all-encompassing words for everything that God made, both seen and unseen. It includes the world of virtues, emotions, and other intangible things, and encompasses the flora and fauna that makes up our normal definition of nature (the lowercase version used to describe the plants and animals outside). You may think an interest in Nature is a given, but these days that is sadly not the case. Many, many people go about their daily lives without any thought or interest in what their environment actually means.

Second, I'm banking on the idea that you know this is a spiritual subject and that we won't be able to talk about Creation being free unless we can acknowledge a spiritual reality to life. Therefore, we'll talk about the reality of angels in the same sentence where we talk about the existence of protons and electrons. Here again, I say this because it is not always something we can take for granted with a reader, as a good portion of the world has forgotten the spiritual origins of all things.

If I can focus this assumption even more, I'm trusting that you know this is a Christ-centered pursuit. I'm hesitant to use the word

"Christian" here because our relationship to our environment has become a hot topic of late all over the world. It is talked about as a *human* issue, and in some respects the Christian church is reluctant to enter into the conversation. But regardless of whether the world ever knows it or not, freeing Creation (on any level) is a function of the work of Jesus, the Christ, and the story God has been presenting to humans since the garden of Eden. The bookends of the Bible are literally the opening and closing chapters of Man's relationship with Creation. As in all things, Christ has the preeminence and has finished the work.

If you read through all of that and checked off all the boxes, then I think we're off to a great start. However, if your friend gave you this book and this is the first time you've ever considered any of this, don't give up just yet. I think I can narrow down my assumptions to one thing – one common denominator that might make someone want to read about this: it's an inward nudge deep in our hearts that tells us there's something unfinished in the story of God, Man, and Creation. And we just can't help ourselves; we want to search it out, and if possible, finish the story.

I was hoping to get to the subject of freeing Creation some years ago when I wrote *Cosmic Shift,* which was another attempt at looking forward in time. Nestled in those chapters about cosmic ages was the issue of commissions – those defining purposes God set forth for each age. I won't go too deeply into it here (I'm trusting you can get a copy if you need to), but as each age changed, so did the commission God gave humanity. And, as you might guess, we stand at the cusp of another shift in cosmic ages at this very moment.

It stands to reason that we are on the verge of inheriting another commission – one that will set the pace for the next chapter of the God/human story. My best guess is that our next commission is the very one the Apostle Paul hinted at in his letter to the Romans.

> *For the creation waits with eager longing for the revealing of the children of God; for the creation was subjected to futility, not of its own*

will but by the will of the one who subjected it, in hope that the creation itself will be set free from its bondage to decay and will obtain the freedom of the glory of the children of God.

– Romans 8: 19 -21 NRSV

It would have a certain symmetry to it as well if this grand story concludes with a commission quite similar to the original one handed to us in Eden. Nevertheless, there just wasn't enough room to go into it in that book, and something as important as this needs its own space. If it helps, though, consider this book the sequel to *Cosmic Shift*, or at least one very long last chapter.

Just between us, there's another reason I didn't include these ideas about restoring Creation in *Cosmic Shift*. I felt I had pushed the reader far enough with (sometimes controversial) ideas about the Mazzaroth (Zodiac), the dawn of the next cosmic age, and the new things we might find out about ourselves and God. I didn't think it would go over very well to also include a whole section claiming that the rocks are alive and that you should talk to them, which is more or less what I'm about to say in the pages to follow. If that piques your interest, then you're in the right place.

Before we really get started, though, I should mention how I've structured this book. It's broken up into three parts. The first part will take you on a journey through history as you rediscover the meaning of myth, paganism, and a Christ-centered restoration of Nature. Bear with me, as that may feel a little academic at times, and some introductory thoughts on poetry may have you a little confused about what that has to do with restoring Nature. Trust me, it's necessary.

Part two will cover the vital tools we'll need to free Creation. In those chapters you'll get a good dose of imagination theory and how we can use that to "see" the spiritual aspects of Nature again.

The final part is my opportunity to tell you what I've experienced in my own life about this subject, and included in those pages are stories of angels and storms, restored myths, and a friendship with Creation that I never knew I could have. That section is without a doubt my favorite part, but it won't make much sense without some established foundations.

Don't get too excited, though. It's not like I've stepped into this role of freeing Creation so thoroughly that every time I walk outside, birds come rest on my shoulder and carry on a conversation. No, I'm not there yet. But I've glimpsed that restored Eden quite a bit over these last years, and from time to time, it presents itself in my earthly sojourn so clearly that I've become convinced this must be the commission we are all about to inherit.

God speed on your journey,
Christopher Paul Carter

Part 1

The Meaning, History, and Relationships of Creation

| 1 |

Amnesia

I liken modern humanity to an amnesiac. That might conjure up the stereotypical image of a person waking up after some severe head trauma and not being able to remember anything before the accident. As a metaphor for our current state, it plays out accurately. There is something that happened a while back that has effectively erased our memory, and we've gotten along pretty well since that event with the knowledge gained from our fresh start.

One might argue (and many, many do) that we're getting along better now than ever. I won't disagree completely, but there'd be no reason to start out this way if I didn't think the voice of our memories is calling out to us in louder and louder tones to recall our origins.

The one major difference between the current state of humanity and an amnesiac is that most amnesiacs know they've lost their past. Normally a doctor is there, after the accident, to tell them what's happened and why they can't remember who they are. Not so for us. We're in the unenviable place of having lost our memories while there was an unfortunate drought of doctors who could tell us what occurred. In other words, we've lost the past, but we're not even aware of it. What do you tell a people who don't know they've lost their memories? How do you tell modern humans that they don't know what they're missing?

It's a challenge, to be sure; but before we get ahead of ourselves, we should narrow down what it is I'm claiming we've forgotten. It just happens to be one of the central issues of the entire Biblical narrative: man's relationship to Creation. That's a broad topic, but that one theme might be secondary only to the overarching Biblical theme of restoration through Christ.

After all, the story begins with a mandate to steward a garden, has in its middle some incredible passages about a restored Creation and every man living under his own vine and fig tree (see both Isaiah and Micah), and concludes with a restored heavens and earth much like the beginning of the story, but even better (Revelation). The redemption of Man and the centrality of Jesus the Christ is for certain the main thing. What Man is supposed to do with that redemption seems to be a really close second.

So, what does this have to do with an amnesiac? Well, the vast majority of human history understood our role in Nature very differently than we do today, and it's not something we talk much about anymore. It's as if we've forgotten the foundational history of understanding Nature.

That only matters – and I want to be very clear about this because the entire argument of this book hangs on it – it only matters if our origins, and how we've viewed Nature throughout history, are essential to knowing how we will fulfill the calling of humanity in the future. If we could do it with just the knowledge we've gained since our "accident" (the one that erased our memories), then there's no need to worry. However, if it's impossible to do it without the wealth of the past, then the subject matter of this book becomes vitally important.

| 2 |

Origins

I've often thought that history and prophecy are the exact same kind of action. One is looking backwards in time while the other looks forward, but they are both looking through *time*. It's as if God gave us these two eyes with which to see our story, and just like the ones on my face, I'm quite fond of both.

We're going back to metaphorical language here, but I've been to the eye doctor quite a bit since my youth, and when the doctor covers up one of your eyes to test the vision of the other, you lose your depth perception. I think this is as good a picture as any to grasp that both history and prophecy should work together in order to provide any depth of understanding of our current state. Take one away and the picture becomes shallow, flat, and less clear.

There are a lot of visions of the future floating around these days, but it's rare to hear of one that accounts for our forgotten history (or even knows we've forgotten something). I'm speaking equally of the two groups who make the most attempts at predicting the future: the scientific and Christian communities. In my view, most of their future-casting falls flat because of the one glaring admission I'm arguing is so important. They try to divine the future without realizing that something happened to us that almost completely eradicated our connection to our ancestors' worldview. It practically ensures that the prophecy will lack any context, and it's the reason I'm wary of anyone who claims to have a picture of the next few hundred years without a good understanding of the previous few hundred.

This book is primarily concerned with the future, and that should explain why I will draw so heavily from the past. In fact, in order to understand the future holistically, I'll go back to the very beginning, the origin of everything – including ourselves – to make a good guess about what will happen next and the role I (or any human) might have in fulfilling it.

Origins are special things. They tell you where you've come from, and that gives your final destination even more meaning. After all, it's the distance between where you began and where you arrive that makes the journey have any meaning at all.

| 3 |

A Stumbling Journey

One thing that should help us all on this journey is a tremendous amount of grace. Here's what I mean: It would be too easy to shout at you, the reader, about how we've all missed the boat and our connection to history has been lost and how we're doomed to misunderstand our future calling in Creation, etc. In other words, I could blame the amnesiac for their condition and make that picture of ourselves the enemy. But that wouldn't help and it's just not appropriate.

First, the process we've gone through that has disconnected us from our past (and by default, our future) is God-ordained. We'll get to that in the chapters ahead. It's not all bad. Nor is the modern era to be scorned. Believe it or not, there are some advantages to being an amnesiac, a fresh start being one of them. And the problems I'm outlining here as the reason for writing this book are no one's fault.

I might get a little testy at what I think are glaring omissions in our education, but you're not to blame for that. And lest I forget, it was some moments of Divine Providence that caused me to stumble into this awareness of our collective amnesia at all. "Stumble" is a good word for it, because I did not know what I was getting myself into just over a decade ago when God started to cure my own amnesia. I've told this story in some way in every book I've written, simply because I owe the content of every book to this one revolutionary experience.

Here's the short version: while comfortably living out my Christian life and doing my best to pursue a close relationship with God, I found myself in a prayer meeting where God decided, without any warning, to open the eyes of my heart (or my spiritual eyes) and show me how the heavenly realm – where Jesus Christ, Himself, ascended to – could be experienced even as I walk out my mortal life.

I believed that realm existed, but I assumed it was off-limits until you die. I was wrong, and I've been devoting my time since that personal revolution to opening as many spiritual eyes as I can. With each passing year this phenomenon becomes a more familiar idea to the average "man on the street." I'm not saying it's common yet, but there are an increasing number of books and other resources out there if you're looking for more testimonies of what I'm describing here.

There's so much to cover about this one topic, and I've written books on the subject so that people can know just how accessible this phenomenon is to every believer, no matter how spiritual we think we are or are not. Please check out some of those other writings if you're unfamiliar with how we are capable of seeing and sensing – some would say "perceiving" – more than just the physical environment of this earthly sojourn.

Again, if this is your first experience with this subject, let me say to you with confidence that you are able to participate with heaven right now! You can be aware of the risen king, Jesus the Christ, as He is seated in the heavenly realms, and should you choose to use the senses God has given, you can make the reality of heaven a part of your everyday life. You are not limited to just this mortal plane. You are capable (commissioned even if you take the Apostle Paul's words literally in 2 Corinthians 4:18) to use your access to heaven right now, as is the right of every citizen of heaven.

We'll talk about those spiritual senses later, because we need them in any attempt to restore Creation, so if you're completely unfamiliar with the claims I just made, and you don't feel like stopping here and reading one of my other books, then just hang on until the later chapters. But let me reiterate that I stumbled upon this blessing that's available to us all. I never expected, not in a million years, that God would open up my spiritual eyes and let me walk around heaven as the Apostle John did in *Revelation.* I would say, just as John did, that I participate in heaven "in the Spirit." I'm very aware that my mortal body is on the earth, but I can be just as aware that I'm communing with God on a heavenly plane.

This incredible side effect of the work of Jesus Christ is becoming increasingly common, but I still feel the need to shout it from the mountaintops. It's just too good a blessing not to share with everyone. The fact that it happened to me without my even searching it out (or knowing it existed) is one reason I believe it's so accessible. Since I didn't do anything to earn it or qualify for it, it must be available to everyone.

It took some years of discovering the heavens to solidify what I will try to convey in this book. But as much as I feel these perspectives are a part of me now, the truth is that I would still be oblivious to them if not for that unasked-for introduction to experiencing heaven. I say all of that to make a point. I've arrived at this place because God likes to bless His kids. All of them. It wasn't because I earned it or somehow had a sense of these things beforehand.

We're all in the same boat here. We're all students, learning those things we never knew we didn't know.

| 4 |

Heroes and Rebels

I'll never forget that first moment I met an angel during one of my times "in the Spirit." I knew it was the beginning of something special. Again, this is a subject I've detailed in other books, and I would recommend reading those to get the whole picture, as the subject of angels is central to a study of Creation. For now, I'll just reiterate how amazing it was to use my spiritual senses to talk with, and get to know, the many angels who seemed as interested in me as I was in them. And as I got to know them, I took note of how each of them seemed to reflect an aspect of the created world. They looked like aspects of Nature, personified.

It was unsettling at first because I knew of no source that could confirm that this was a true picture of the angelic world. In fact, at one point I was sure that I would never be able to speak of the watery angels, the ones made of fire, the angels of light, or the virtues to anyone lest they think I was crazy. In all of my Christian years, not one person, pastor, or theologian ever made mention of a connection between angels and the entirety of Nature all around us. This just isn't something they teach you in Sunday school.

So, I kept it to myself, and privately enjoyed discovering a world of spirits in Nature. That is, until the day heaven had me stumble onto a teacher who convinced me I wasn't crazy, but rather, I was seeing the world as humanity would have seen it before their amnesia.

How that happened is a story worth telling. There were a few books I was reading through simultaneously. One was a summary of some influential ideas in the field of physics called *Physics for the Rest of Us,* and the other was a book called *Celtic Christianity: Ecology and Holiness.* Anyone who knows me might have a chuckle at this point, because these two books encapsulate my interests quite well. I earned my degree in physics, and that's still a lens through which I see the world. At the same time, I'm continually drawn to the Celtic (or better yet, Gaelic) expressions of the Christian faith. Those two books, which anyone would swear are vastly different subjects, kept referencing the same author: Owen Barfield.

The physics book quoted his work *Saving the Appearances,* while *Celtic Christianity* had an endorsement from Barfield on the back cover. I was stunned. How could these two very different books pull from the same source? How does someone influence both of these subjects? To me, it was a mystery I had to uncover, as those two subjects paint a perfect picture of my own influences: equal parts physics and Celtic Christianity. Anyone who spanned that gap had something very important to impart to me.

I started to read *Saving the Appearances,* but within the first few chapters I was in over my head. I had stepped into the world of a philosopher who had forgotten more about the story of Man than I had ever learned. It took three readings before I felt I grasped what Owen Barfield was trying to say. But finally, I had found a voice that could make sense of what I had been doing in the heavens for the previous years. Owen Barfield's teachings gave me the language to talk about my own experiences.

He helped me understand why I saw angels the way I did. He gave me context, through history, about what was happening to me and why the opening of my spiritual eyes was so important. He provided the vocabulary to talk about our changing relationship with Nature. I dare say it was his words that finally helped me to understand the Apostle Paul's prophecy in Romans, chapter 8, that you read earlier. His contributions to every part of this book, even these introductory paragraphs, cannot be overstated.

If you've read *Saving the Appearances,* or any other of Barfield's works, then you'll feel the influences of his ideas throughout this entire book. As I walk you through the Scientific Revolution and how it changed our spiritual perceptions, or when I use the term *participation,* or when we discuss the role of imagination in all of this, those are all due to Barfield's language and ethos. This one paragraph can't do it justice, but it will have to suffice as my attempt to give him all the credit he deserves. This book simply would not exist without his giant contribution.

There are a few other things for which I need to thank Owen Barfield. His books settled me on this journey, and I can't tell you, dear Reader, how much it meant to me to learn that I was not the *only one,* that my experiences were not the first of their kind, and that my perceptions were rooted in something far bigger than myself. Furthermore, finding this anchor in Owen Barfield opened the door to other teachers who were about the same business of awakening humanity to the drastic changes in our consciousness that have occurred in the last few centuries.

Through Barfield, I discovered the Romantic poets – rebels in their own right – who fought the industrialization of our minds and held firm to the belief in a spiritual world. In fact, I owe all aspects of my own rediscovery of poetry to him, as I never would have considered it as anything more than just fancy language.

At one point, I imagined writing this book as a sort of "*Saving the Appearances* in laymen's terms." Lots of people have picked up Barfield's books only to be completely lost a few chapters in. I thought it would help to translate Barfield to a generation who might not have the time or prerequisite knowledge to decipher what he meant (and I'm still not sure I know). So, think of this as my own personal rewrite of what he taught me, mixed with a heavy dose of my own experiences.

One last note: many people have been thankful for Owen Barfield's wisdom, one of them being the beloved C.S. Lewis, who called Barfield "the wisest and best of my unofficial teachers."

| 5 |

Creation Poetry

I'll be honest, I never really liked poetry. Studying it in school was a chore, and Shakespeare's sonnets hurt my brain. But poetry, like so many ancient and original things, needs a rediscovery. I'm sure some readers are delighted to read about poetic origins; but for most people, poetry was something you trudged through in school and have purposefully avoided since. A quick description of poetry (and we need one today) can be best accomplished by comparing it to prose.

Prose is the form of writing that you are reading right now, and it is a good way to explain things. With prose (again, think of this book), I can use as many words as I need in a straightforward way to get my thoughts out, which is normally needed to make something understandable. Poetry, on the other hand, has a different economy of words. It employs only the best words to say something, and then frames them with things like meter and rhyme. Sometimes, given these additional elements, I think of poetry as language with more dimensions, since it isn't just straightforward talk. There's something about poetry that works beyond our objective mind. In a way, poetry is written from a *deeper* place, and it can be almost supernatural in the way it reveals meaning and purpose.

Did you know that most of the earliest examples of writing we have unearthed to date are some form of poetry? The further back we go in literature, we find less and less prose and more and more poetry, until we've arrived at a point in history where it's all just poetry. It's as if the origin of writing *was* poetry.

Many scholars have considered the connection between literature and thought and how they have developed simultaneously. If you buy into that (and I do), then it's a short leap to the following conclusion: since the earliest forms of literature are poetry, humanity's earliest thoughts must have been poetic. Try not to think of a nursery rhyme here, but rather of a kind of language that conveys the inner sense of things. The essence. The spirit. The meaning.

A significant portion of the Bible (about a third) is poetry. In fact, the very first chapter of Genesis, which covers the beginning of everything, was written in poetic form. Far from a prosaic, modern history book, Genesis, chapter 1, was that same kind of original language that was so adept at establishing meaning. And that meaning has been lost to the man on the street for a long time.

What something *means* is not a question science is good at answering. And, like it or not, we all see the world through a scientific lens. We tend to read the first chapter of Genesis with an eye toward how God made the objects and matter all around us, kind of like a scientist would. But that's not the question that occupied the mind of someone thousands of years ago. To an ancient reader, Genesis was never about scientific questions. But it had a lot to say about *why* we are here. Even more, it answered the questions, "What are we?" and "What is God?" and "What is everything else?"

As stated before, origins are important. I'd venture a guess that God started with these issues because they were the most important foundations for a full human life. In other words, it may not matter how much we know about "matter," if we don't know who we are and what our role is in this vast, wonderful Cosmos. And if you had lived back in an ancient time, this poem, with its seven days of Creation, was designed to get you to think of something else that took seven days to complete – the inauguration of a temple.

| 6 |

The Cosmic Temple

Ancient civilizations took temple building very seriously. Oftentimes it was the center of life, even more so than any governmental structure or palace. Regardless of how long it took to build one, the temple didn't become a temple until it was consecrated or inaugurated. Until then it was just raw materials that had been hammered into place. It took a special ceremony or celebration to begin its function as a place where humanity and deity could meet. Often the ancient literature that described the creation of a temple used the same seven-day model as Genesis, chapter 1.

Think of this as a worldview that the ancient Near East took for granted, even if it's foreign to us today. To them, it was a simple fact that temples were ceremonially established in seven days. This is not to say that the Creation poem in Genesis borrowed from other cultures or that those other cultures took these ideas from the Bible. It's simply the way they saw the world. And the pervasiveness of a seven-day inauguration in ancient Near East temple literature should tell us that the ancient world shared some common knowledge about what temples really are. Simply put, the design of the poem in Genesis was a familiar design to the ancient world. It was supposed to get them thinking of a temple.

To further the comparison, God rests on day number seven, after the work of Creation had finished. The idea of God "resting" in a place is literally the reason all temples were built in the ancient world. The temple was a house for God (or whatever lower-case god for whom it was built), and it was believed that the deity's presence *rested* in that place. So, not only do we see the same seven-day pattern in the literature of Genesis as we do in other ancient Near East temple accounts, but we also see God doing what all other deities were believed to do in a temple: Rest, live, and dwell there.

For all the ancient ears that heard it, the design of this Hebrew poem was meant to convey the meaning, Creation = Temple. We might need a minute to connect these dots, because reading the Creation account as a temple inauguration is not something we normally talk about. It helps to be reminded that God chose to tell the Creation story in a specific kind of seven-day poem that meant something special to the world that first heard it. God doesn't do things arbitrarily, so we at least need to consider the meanings inherent in this kind of literature.

Bible scholars have been unearthing the relationship of the seven days of Creation recorded in Genesis to the seven days of a temple inauguration for a while. *The Lost World of Genesis One,* a book by John H. Walton, does a great job of revealing the historical records of seven-day temple inaugurations. If you're interested in those details, and which cultures followed those practices, I would highly recommend his scholarly approach.

Walton, along with many other sources like BibleProject.com, have done much to highlight how the Hebrew temple (and many other temples of the ancient world) were designed to look like the original temple of Creation – Nature – in all its wonder. The ceiling of the temple was the sky and the decorations on the walls emulated plants. There was even a menorah in the temple with seven lights. Interestingly, there are seven moving lights in the sky that are visible to our naked eye (Sun, Moon, and five observable planets). In all respects, temples were designed to look like a symbol of the Cosmos, itself. Or, perhaps they were all modeling the perfect God/Man meeting space – the garden of Eden.

> *We can draw the connection between temple and cosmos more tightly when we observe that temples in the ancient world were considered symbols of the cosmos. (page 78, The Lost World of Genesis One)*

Walton's research gives us some other useful historical tidbits about the Genesis poem. For instance, the verbs used in Genesis for "create" are descriptive words for establishing purposes and functions more than the creation of physical material. While no one reading that poem would have ever questioned that God made the actual, physical stuff of the Cosmos, the poem was there to explain the purpose of each part of Nature in the same way a purpose was established for each article and design in a temple.

It was God's way of saying that all of Nature – all of its beauty and form and function – was all designed to create a space where God's Presence can be related to and accessed. It was God's way of saying, "Do you see everything that's out there? This whole Cosmos is the house of my Presence." Because of this, I think it's very easy to begin calling Nature the "Cosmic Temple," a term John H. Walton uses. Think about what temples are for. They are purposeful spaces where mankind can connect spiritual things to earthly things. God to Man. Life to Meaning.

The next time you walk outside on a breezy afternoon or ponder a starry night, try to see everything around you as one massive cathedral designed to house God's Presence and connect it to the world of Man. Imagine that spiritually active world for a moment. Would it change the way we thought of the stars, oceans, virtues, and plants if we saw each part with a spiritual meaning? Would we see them as part of our connection to God, just as the ancients saw a temple?

Remember, to our ancestors, a temple was the dwelling place of God. Even pagan temples were believed to house a deity of one kind or another. When you entered a temple, you were entering a specific structure that was designed to hold that deity's presence. All the attributes of the temple were specifically made for the purposes of ministering to that deity. And, in the case of the temple and tabernacle of the Old Testament, it was a structure where mankind and God could meet – even face to face. These are the kinds of ideas Genesis, chapter 1, was supposed to instill when it was written many millennia ago.

| 7 |

You Are a Mirror

Now that we are reminded that the Cosmos was created to be a temple, then our next questions might be, "What is mankind?" "Why are we in the temple, too?" Your first thought might be that mankind is the priest of this temple, because every temple needs someone to manage and take care of its forms and functions. That's a good and true start, and we certainly see humans doing that job in ancient history. But it doesn't explain everything about the special nature of humanity, and it certainly doesn't capture the real scandal of the first chapter of Genesis (scandalous only because it places such immense value and importance on humanity when compared with other ancient creation stories).

Humankind was the only part of Creation that was made specifically in God's image and likeness. Consider that a way to understand the phrase "image and likeness" is the word "reflection," which holds true to the original Hebrew meaning of the word. Being made in God's reflection – like a mirror image – would mean that humans were the physical presence of Deity in the temple. It's as if God put bits and pieces of God's self in the creation of mankind to walk around and be the presence of God in the Cosmic Temple.

The "scandal" of all of this becomes apparent when we connect the dots again between Creation and a temple. In the cultures of the ancient world, a temple was built to house a deity, and that deity was represented in an idol. The idol could have been a simple clay or metal statue, or something like the towering image of Athena in the Greek Parthenon. However, this practice is notably absent from the inauguration of the Cosmic Temple in Genesis. After all, God does not make an idol of God's self to put in the garden of Eden... or does He?

The Hebrew word for "image" can also be translated "idol." That's right, when God said, "Let us make man in our image," it's the same word that gets translated into the word "idol" elsewhere. I understand why Bible translators chose a different word there, but it leaves out how scandalous and ground-breaking Genesis really is.

The claim being made is that God didn't put an idol in the Cosmic Temple because *Man* is the idol of God's Presence. It's a profound understanding of human nature, and it's where Genesis stands apart from any other creation literature the world over. Think about this for a few moments more. You owe it to yourself. In every temple of the ancient world, there was an idol representing a god. In the Cosmic Temple of Genesis, chapter 1, God self-forms an idol called mankind and sets that image in the temple to represent the Godhead. The next time you look in the mirror, try to grapple a bit more with your role as the image – or idol – of God in this world.

As an aside, there are multiple layers of how much temple functions play out in the Biblical narrative. The New Testament adds the notion that we are also a kind of temple in and of ourselves, as if there is a God-temple in each human, who then is called to represent God within the larger temple called the Cosmos. I think the structure of the Old Testament tabernacle and temple could shed a lot of light on what a temple within a temple looks like, since there was a special "Holy of Holies" inside the greater temple structure with its inner and outer courts.

Do you not know that you are God's temple and that God's Spirit dwells in you?

– 1 Corinthians 3: 16

I wonder what kind of elevating thoughts must have occurred in the minds of early mankind simply by reading God's Creation poem? Or just think of what it meant to the Hebrews of the Old Testament to contemplate this Creation account that places man at the center of God's work, even in God's image, while the rest of the world bowed down to idols made of clay.

I've heard it said that when poetry is well written or "done right," as it were, it causes a change in consciousness. It moves you. After hearing it, you're not the same. I think of poetry, especially in its ancient forms, as a type of language that communicates beyond the veil between this world and the heavens. Or should I say it "connects" this world and the heavens, since it pulls meanings from a spiritual origin into this physical world?

Is it any wonder that God used poetry to describe the creation of the Cosmic Temple? Is it any wonder that it took a spiritual kind of language to convey the meaning of mankind? God is using this poem to bring things from a spiritual plane into this world of incarnation. Poetry may be the only kind of language that has the power to do that.

If thinking about poetry and the history of language this way seems odd, perhaps we've touched on something that was well known to our ancestors but somehow forgotten by us – that certain kinds of language have a spiritual power all their own. Interestingly, the same event that changed the way we see Nature is also responsible for our losing the power (or meaning) of poetry. But let's not get too far ahead. We've just seen what the Genesis poem meant to someone thousands of years ago, and my hope is that understanding the Cosmos as a temple will get you thinking more spiritually about Nature. In fact, in the eyes of our ancestors, Nature did not just *have* spiritual meaning… it *was* spiritual.

| 8 |

What Is a Star?

If you've ever read a science book about the stars, then you know, technically, what they are. Well, maybe. We know from our modern, scientific understanding that stars are supposed to be giant, luminescent balls of gas, sometimes an incalculable distance away from us. They're so far away that we have to measure the distance in light-years. That's the distance covered in one year if you were moving at the speed of light. But is that all they are?

Inside these stars, we've been taught that hydrogen is becoming helium in a process called nuclear fusion. It releases a lot of energy, which explains all the light and heat. These facts about stars are things we take for granted. It is practically unquestioned today. But does that tell us everything there is to know about stars? Does that tell us everything we *should* know about them?

I'm reminded of a favorite book of mine, *The Voyage of the Dawn Treader,* by C.S. Lewis. There's a point in the story where one of the characters makes this very assumption, that our modern notion of a star is all that there is to know. I'll give you a snippet of the conversation between the character Eustace and the being called Ramandu, who was a "retired star," as Lewis puts it.

> "In our world," said Eustace, "a star is a huge ball of flaming gas."
>
> "Even in your world, my son, that is not what a star is but only what it is made of."

Right there, in C.S. Lewis's famous children's book, we are faced with this dilemma – that there is a difference between knowing the objective facts about something versus knowing what it really is. To know something objectively is to know just the outside of something. What could be hidden away on the inside of the Cosmos if we dared to look?

Today, most people would not hesitate to say that they knew what stars were. We would even say we knew them well if we knew all the facts about them. Their color, temperature, lifespan, location, etc. But apply that to a human being. If you know all the outward facts about a human being, do you really know that person? Doesn't it take more than objective definitions to understand a person made in God's image? If I just know your size, color, and location, do I really know you?

Obviously not. There's much more to you than that, but most people would say that stars, or any part of Nature for that matter, don't deserve the same treatment. Most modern people would say that stars are *just* objects, with no inner quality to discover.

Owen Barfield referred to this kind of thinking as a "dashboard knowledge" of Nature. To illustrate the point, ask yourself if you have to know how a car works in order to drive one. Almost everyone I know would laughingly say, "No." Most of us have no idea how the modern car starts up, runs, adjusts the air temperature, or tunes into a radio signal, to say nothing of how it can pair to your cell phone to play music or answer calls.

All of this becomes painfully apparent when something goes wrong and we have to take it to the shop, where someone knows something about it and can fix it. Aren't you always a little nervous when you go? Aren't you always wondering if the mechanic is telling you the truth?

We feel this way because many of us don't know anything about it and the mechanic could say anything and we'd never be the wiser. I doubt most car mechanics are deserving of this suspicion. It's simply a result of our insecurity born out of our ignorance.

The point Barfield was making, and this will come up a lot as we go on, is that it's entirely possible to work something – to use it – without knowing how it really works. In other words, you can know something on the surface and even make it do your will without understanding at all what it really is (or what its true purpose is). To go back to our example, you can turn the steering wheel and read the gauges on the dashboard without having any knowledge of internal combustion engines or electrical displays. You make it work for you, even if you don't know how it works.

Such is the state of modern humanity. We have a grasp of how to use Nature objectively, and we've gone so far down that road that we don't even consider that there's more of Nature to know beyond just the "dashboard knowledge." However, every one of our ancestors started with the notion that stars – and Nature – had personality. That's the "inner" knowledge that today we call mythic. The objective facts came much, much later. When we're done with this trip, let's ask ourselves if a star is only a "huge ball of flaming gas"? While we're at it, we might as well ask ourselves if any part of Creation can be fully defined by just the outward facts.

| 9 |

The Nature of Myth

Mythology is a study of the stories of the distant past. Think of all the gods and goddesses of various cultures, or perhaps the stories of demi-gods and human heroes. You could also include creatures and animals that defy explanation, like dragons, centaurs, and fairies. It's all included in the study of myths.

What we think about those myths today is very different from what our ancestors thought. And most modern people don't really question why our views have changed so much – or even that there has been a change – so distant are these memories of Man's beginnings in the Cosmic Temple. But there is one thing we must understand before we go on: The ancient world viewed these myths as part of their story. To them it wasn't fiction or fairy tales. It was history.

Our modern notion of the myths is that they were, at best, metaphors and, at worst, hallucinations. For instance, we can imagine a learned writer creating stories out of thin air about humans interacting with cosmic spiritual beings to make a moral or philosophical point. But we can't imagine that same writer claiming that the events of the far-fetched story actually happened. If the writer were saying *that,* then we would claim the writer was plumb crazy and suffering from a delusion. We've created a category for myths today that means anything but "this story actually happened."

The Merriam-Webster dictionary definition of the word "myth" is "an unfounded or false notion." That definition is a great way to see our modern dismissal of mythology. It has actually created a definition of myth that means "not true." Interestingly, stories like Noah's ark and the great flood are also considered to be myths in our modern world. For that matter, the entirety of Genesis through the story of the Tower of Babel in chapter 11 is often seen the same way.

When speaking of the ancients' way of perceiving stories we would now call myth, we're talking about a perspective reaching back to a time before what we would even call "history." A word for this period would be "prehistory" because it describes a world and its events in a way that defies our modern categories. Put simply, we don't understand "prehistory," so we don't want to call it "history."

To the modern reader, it just seems like a completely different world. A world where angels can guard the way to an eternal garden, where spiritual beings can (and regularly do) descend from the heavens to interact with mankind, and where humans can build structures that open doors to the heavens (like the story of the Tower of Babel). It all sounds like fantasy, science fiction, or myth... to *us*. Again, to our ancestors, it was a perfect description of their own origins.

| 10 |

Giants

Let's see how our understanding of myth plays out in a Biblical sense. For instance, do you believe in giants?

> *And the Lord said, "My Spirit shall not strive with man forever, for he is indeed flesh; yet his days shall be one hundred and twenty years." There were giants [Nephilim] on the earth in those days, and also afterward, when the sons of God came in to the daughters of men and they bore children to them. Those were the mighty men who were of old, men of renown.*
>
> *– Genesis 6: 3 -4 NKJV*

Here, in Genesis, chapter 6, a story of mythological proportions is taking place, and any reader has to make a choice. Did this really happen? Did beings from the heavens descend to earth and produce a hybrid offspring? Or, is it some kind of metaphor or allegory meant to teach a moral or philosophical lesson?

The problem with treating this as a metaphor ("metaphor" means not literal, but rather symbolic or representative) is that it allows us to treat any seemingly unbelievable part of Scripture in the same way. But wait, isn't the entire Bible supernatural in nature? Isn't the foundation of Christianity a faith in this supernatural narrative? If we begin to apply a metaphorical lens to the parts of the Bible we've decided aren't to be taken seriously, simply because it seems unbelievable to us, then we give ourselves the freedom to do that with any part, even the foundations of the gospel.

For instance, is the story of Jesus multiplying the fishes and loaves to feed thousands of people any more explainable? Or what about Jesus' resurrection from the dead? You can see how easy it is to dismiss something in the Bible from being an actual fact if it doesn't fit into our modern worldview. My point is if we believe the miracles and resurrection of Jesus (and I hope you do), then we must also believe the rest of the Bible when it shows us something equally otherworldly.

In Genesis 6, there is a mention of the "Herculean" stories common in Greek mythology. We are told of "men of renown," and some translations will render it "heroes of old." Apparently, even the Bible gets in on telling the stories of prehistory, as these phrases call to mind mythic, demi-god heroes like Theseus and Perseus. The general storyline is the same. A god descends to earth and produces a kind of hybrid offspring. The earliest interpretation of the phrase "sons of God" was "angels" of God.

We're literally talking about spiritual beings (or angels, we can use the terms interchangeably) coming from the heavens to procreate with humans! Sound like the demi-god myths of old? But the difference here is that the Bible presents this union between the sons of God and humans as a very bad thing. Even the word for "giants" in Hebrew is the word "Nephilim." It means "fallen ones." And if the word "giants" is the best way to read this passage, then we have one more similarity between this passage and the myriad myths of giants throughout the world.

Again, we have a choice here. We can pick and choose which parts of the Biblical narrative are true, and cast away those things we find too outlandish. Or we can accept that it's giving us a clear view of history that even validates something like the unholy mating of fallen spiritual beings (fallen angels masquerading as gods) with humanity found in the "myths" (or prehistories) of many cultures.

Just like the idea of a seven-day temple inauguration, the notion of spiritual beings actively present in our world is something that ancient people took for granted. Hebrew or Gentile, the entire ancient world believed the "gods" of mythology were real, even if they saw them from different perspectives.

It's an interesting subject to be sure, but the reason why myth is important in a study of Nature is two-fold. First, if myth means something other than "not true," then we have to consider it as a valid part of our human memory. Perhaps it can go into a category of history when mankind was primarily concerned with recording the spiritual events of the world. We'll get into why the modern world discounts that later. The second reason has to do with the nature of those gods (or fallen angels) immortalized in myth. Without exception, every deity of the ancient world was associated with a part of Nature.

| 11 |

Our Original Participation

I grew up thinking that ancient cultures imagined spiritual beings inhabiting parts of Nature because that was the best way they had to explain how the world worked. That simple premise goes something like this: because ancient peoples didn't have science to explain how the rain falls, they needed to imagine a spirit that inhabited and controlled the weather. Because they didn't understand how babies were born, plants grew, crystals formed, eclipses occurred, or mountains erupted with lava, they needed to invent unseen agents that would explain all the unexplained activity of Nature.

That's what we believe gave birth to Zeus with his storms, Poseidon with his earthquakes, and Aphrodite with her romance. The modern world calls this "animism," but in the chapters to follow you'll understand why that term has only been around since the advent of science.

Every modern mind is probably ingrained with this set of beliefs about the ancient world. We all think their view of Nature – inhabited by spiritual beings – was their best guess at how things worked, as if they were also looking for the dashboard knowledge that the modern world craves but were kept ignorant by their superstitions. We believe they were all misguided or just too simple to understand what we've deemed is most important (and the only truth worth considering). We think of ourselves as more learned and complete, and so we don't need to see (or, if you will, imagine) the spirits in Nature as they did. In short, we believe they didn't understand or perceive *as well* as we do today.

It's surprising that we're willing to discount such a large portion of human history as fanciful delusions born out of ignorance. We're talking about thousands of years of human history, gone in a flash, and dismissed out of hand as irrelevant.

And there's a second learned bias here: even if someone did find value in the ancient world's view of Nature, the Bible and Christian faith are here to clear all that up, right? Don't we believe that their worldview is simply the work of paganism and not a "proper" Christian worldview? So, it's fine for the pagan myths to imagine a spiritual being inhabiting the oceans, mountains, and stars, but surely the Bible tells us that Nature is just lifeless (or at least spiritless) objects... or does it?

Go and read Psalm 104 (in the New International Version), where God makes "winds His angels." Rediscover that fire is called one of God's ministering spirits. Hear the passages that tell of the stars speaking to us night after night (Psalm 19). And take into account the moments when Jesus talked to the storm and the Apostle John saw an angel in the sun (the Gospels and Revelation, respectively).

Far from finding a Bible that sets the record straight and contradicts a spiritually alive view of Nature, we instead are gripped by a Hebrew history, a Messiah, and an early church that is as aware of the spiritual origins of Nature as their pagan neighbors. The only difference – and it's a big one – is that they didn't worship those spiritual beings as God. Their existence, however, was never doubted.

You can probably already see where I'm going with this. It seems unlikely to me that we can discover our future commission concerning Nature if we discredit our original comprehension of it. And, I'll go ahead and give the disclaimer now that we do not need to diminish our scientific worldview in order to do that. It's important that we know that weather is caused by temperature and pressure changes, that lava erupts from a mountain because of plate tectonics, and that the mystery of birth is begun in a tiny meeting of sperm and egg. Our knowledge today, born of science, is important. But it's not more important than the knowledge of our ancestors, or of Christ Himself!

I mean, who talks to the wind and waves anymore? Or trees? Or who hears God's voice in the thunder? These are all recorded activities of Jesus Christ, and I think it's safe to assume He knew something of how the world really worked. It doesn't matter where we look in the ancient world, we're going to find the same picture of Nature, and that leaves us with only two options: Either the entire ancient world, which includes Jesus Christ, is misguided and uninformed, or there's more to Nature than we've ever considered. I'll suggest once again, maybe we've simply forgotten.

This doesn't mean that our view today, absent of any spiritual presence in Nature, is wrong. It just means we've been looking at something very differently. We've been looking at the objects of nature – just the physical stuff of matter and how it fits together. The ancient world was looking at these things, too. But they were also observing the spirit of Nature, which seemed to be a much more pertinent issue to all those who came before us.

I think this is a good time to get rid of terms like "right" and "wrong" as we discuss our perception of Nature. Instead, let's talk of our ancestors' ideas and observations as "original," since they are the foundations of our Nature understanding. We need not make the claim that their view or comprehension was complete, only that it was real. And we can speak from here on about our "original participation" with Nature.

What I mean by that (and this is a Barfield idea again) is interacting with Nature as the outer forms of an inner spiritual reality is the first way mankind learned to participate with our environment. Participation simply means to take part in something, to contribute, to share with, and to engage. In this context it implies giving and taking. It's reciprocal.

Our original participation with light, for example, wasn't with the dual wave/particle nature of the electromagnetic spectrum. It was with a spiritual being who *is* the light. Our first impressions of Earth's waters weren't with two hydrogen atoms bonded with one oxygen atom, it was with a spirit who gave form and voice to those beautiful and terrible waves. Our first notion of the stars wasn't one of flaming balls of gas millions of miles away. It was of a vast, heavenly, angelic host whom God commissioned to speak to the Earth.

In our first picture of the world, all this natural wonder was alive. And it was there to pour into humanity, as the image of God, just as the materials of a temple were designed to house the idol of God's Presence. And, reciprocally, the representation of God is what gave meaning and purpose to all the articles and functions of the Cosmic Temple. Unless the Presence of God is there, the objects would just be objects.

In the Biblical narrative, this original state of the Cosmic Temple lasted for just two chapters or so. What we call the "Fall of Man" happens in chapter 3 of Genesis. However, this first state of Man and Nature left such an impression on us that it carried our worldview through over 5,000 years of human development. You read that right, the vast majority of human history has been lived in a state of what can be called original participation with Nature. You can still hear it in the writings of some early Christian leaders:

St. Augustine, who lived in the 4th century A.D., said,

> I do not think you can step on a blade of grass without touching an angel.

The Rune of St. Patrick, the famous 4th century Irish apostle, reverberates with a spiritual Nature. Here you can see Patrick calling the parts of the Cosmic Temple to help him in his work:

> *At Tara today in this fateful hour*
> *I place all heaven with its power,*
> *and the sun with its brightness,*
> *and the snow with its whiteness,*

and fire with all the strength it hath,
and lightning with its rapid wrath,
and the winds with their swiftness along their path,
and the sea with its deepness,
and the rocks with their steepness
and the earth with its starkness:
all these I place,
by God's almighty help and grace,
between myself and the powers of darkness.

Another voice of original participation is St. Francis of Assisi, who lived around 1,200 years after Jesus walked the earth. The stories of his life and his supernatural relationship with birds and animals suggest he was well on his way to freeing Creation. Here is his *Canticle of Brother Sun*:

All praise be yours, my Lord,
through all, you have made, and first, my lord Brother Sun, who brings the day;
and through whom you give us light.

How beautiful is he, how radiant in all his splendor;
Of you, Most High, he bears the likeness.
All Praise be yours, my Lord, through Sister Moon
and the stars; in the heavens you have made them, bright, and precious, and fair.

All praise be yours, my Lord,
through Brothers wind and air, and fair and stormy, all the weather's moods,

by which you cherish all that you have made.
All praise be yours, my Lord, through Sister Water,

So useful, humble, precious and pure.
All praise be yours, my Lord, through Brother Fire,
through whom you brighten up the night. How beautiful is he, how cheerful!
Full of power and strength.

All praise be yours, my Lord, through our Sister
Mother Earth, who sustains us and governs us,
and produces various fruits with colored flowers and herbs.

All praise be yours, my Lord,
through those who grant pardon for love of you;
through those who endure sickness and trial.

Happy are those who endure in peace,
By You, Most High, they will be crowned.
All praise be yours, my Lord, through Sister Death,

From whose embrace no mortal can escape.
Woe to those who die in mortal sin!
Happy those she finds doing your will! The second death can do them no harm.
Praise and bless my Lord, and give him thanks
And serve him with great humility.

As I've said before, origins are special things. Where we begin has a lot to do with where we end up, and it helps us to see where we went astray as well.

| 12 |

Paganism

There's a dark side to original participation, and it's at least one reason why some folks distrust these ideas. I brought it up casually earlier, but most people know that much of recorded human history spoke of spirits in Nature as gods. They were worshiped.

The Hebrew Bible works in the same general worldview, but separates itself by steering humanity away from other gods and towards the Most High God, in whose image they were made. However, the vast majority of myths were recorded by Gentile cultures who believed the pagan gods reigned supreme. So what happened? What changed to make this perfect Cosmic Temple turn into a deceived mess? Enter into the story an interaction with Nature that didn't go well at all.

The Bible records this moment in Genesis, chapter 3, and it's often called the "Fall of Man." But using our historical eyes, we might also call it the "Fall of Nature." Adam and Eve were tempted to do something that God said would result in their death (and it did), and this "fall" was instigated by a spiritual being who appeared in the form of a serpent. This original antagonist is sometimes called "Satan," which means "accuser" or "adversary." The book of Revelation connects the dots for us between the serpent in the garden and the evil force we've called the Devil (and it's always interesting to see the how the end of the Bible reflects the beginning).

And the great dragon was thrown down, the serpent of old who is called the devil and Satan, who deceives the whole world; he was thrown down to the earth, and his angels were thrown down with him.

– Revelation 12: 9 NASB

A common spiritual view would hold that Satan and his fallen angels are spiritual beings, opposing God's work and generally trying to derail humanity from God's purposes. Seen through the eyes of original participation, Satan and the fallen spirits are also directly connected to aspects of Creation.

Have you wondered what part of Nature Satan might have personified? The name gives it away. A common name for the Devil, "Lucifer," comes from the Hebrew "heilel ben shakhar," which is taken from Isaiah, chapter 14. "Lucifer" means "light bearer." Heilel ben shakhar, means "shining light or brightness born of the dawn." You're probably getting the "light" theme here. When the Devil (Satan, Heilel, Lucifer) fell, he no longer personified God's light. He had become a perverse darkness, hence the moniker "prince of darkness."

There are some other Biblical references connecting Satan to a fallen cherub, one of the powerful creatures surrounding God's throne. Again, the idea is that he was once holy, beautiful, and powerful. When he fell, he became a perversion of what he was created to be, and he took a portion of the Cosmic Temple with him. In the eyes of our ancestors, Nature fell *with* humanity. Or maybe it was the other way around.

Either way, the corruption of humanity and the corruption of Nature occurred at about the same time. They both fell. From this point in human history onward, not every spiritual being inhabiting a part of Nature was for our good. At least one led the way in this path to corruption, but he was accompanied by many others who were happy to join in this work of deceiving mankind. You've probably already guessed it, but these fallen spirits are the so-called gods and goddesses of every pagan culture.

We should take a moment to imagine life in the Cosmic Temple when it was fully perfect and incorruptible, just to get some perspective. No part of Nature would do harm to humanity, and vice versa. Existence was mutually beneficial and reciprocal for everyone present in the garden of Eden. Perhaps Adam and Eve could talk to the animals, the trees, the sky, and the stars just as easily as we talk to each other today.

Now imagine taking a path that led away from that idyllic state into a place where Nature and mankind were suddenly at odds with each other. Imagine being afraid of animals for the first time or being burnt by too much sun. Could it be that the first bite from a poisonous spider was a big surprise? On a smaller scale, imagine encountering a swarm of mosquitoes and having to deal with the knowledge that a part of Nature has suddenly decided to feed on *YOU.*

These are everyday occurrences to us, but they are all part of a human experience that has fallen from its original state. It's important to note here that humanity and Creation are locked together in their fates. One didn't fall without the other, which means a restoration would be two-fold as well. As we move to that moment of future restoration, consider all the parts of Creation that seem like a perversion of something good.

Consider both the butterfly and the mosquito. One is welcomed and the other hated. Perhaps the butterfly with its beautiful wings and gentle curling proboscis that drinks nectar from flowers is a picture of how Nature should be. In contrast, the mosquito drinks human (and animal) blood from its own, ready-made hypodermic needle of a mouth. One is beautiful, the other can look almost skeletal (I've lived a lot in the southern United States, so I've clearly thought about this). Now imagine a holy angel contrasted with an evil spirit. See the resemblance to the butterfly and the mosquito? We can see all around us the evidence that parts of Nature have fallen into corruption.

In the same way, we can think of paganism as the corruption of original participation. It's the natural result of what happens when fallen spiritual beings personifying corrupted parts of Nature decide to rule over mankind. And this was the condition of most of humanity for literally thousands of years (and still is in many places and cultures). "Pagan" means "believing in many gods," and to most of the world, these fallen spirits were part of a host of deities controlling certain aspects of the Cosmic Temple. I'll use the Greek, Roman, and Egyptian names here since most people are familiar with them, but this worldview was repeated everywhere.

Ra was the god of the Sun. Zeus was the sky and the storm, and the king of the Greek pantheon of gods. Neptune was the deity of the seas. Saturn personified time and agriculture. Aphrodite gave voice to some intangible parts of Creation like love and beauty. These names, "Neptune, Ra, Aphrodite," are the proper names humankind learned for these very real fallen angels. They're just as real as the proper names Michael and Gabriel, two angelic names from the Hebrew Bible.

Zeus and Neptune certainly had their tempers and seemed to take advantage of human women to produce their offspring (sound familiar, Nephilim?). If mankind didn't worship them the right way, they would get mad. Saturn (or Cronus) was famous for eating his children so they wouldn't one day overpower him. And Aphrodite... well, let's just say that the corruption of love and beauty looks a lot like lust and vanity and leave it at that. The pagan world was certainly interesting, and it gave us some great perspective on man's early relationship with the fallen world, but thank God this wasn't the end of the story.

When Jesus confronted the wind and the waves, He was reminding this fallen part of the temple that the image of God was back, and that things were going to change. He spoke to the wind, rebuked it even, in the same way He would a person who could both hear His words and accept His correction. And why wouldn't He? As mentioned before, the Psalms said the winds were a kind of angel, and mythology tells us of many spirit beings sensed in the wind and storm. Had the spirit personifying the storm in this instance been holy, it would not have needed a rebuke from the Messiah. Had the waves here been in agreement with God's original design, He would not have had to firmly correct them.

Given that the spirit who personified storms in Greek history was Zeus, or in his Canaanite form, Baal, it's fun to imagine Jesus taking the king of the fallen pantheon to task and telling him, "Quiet down, you're scaring the disciples." It's a powerful scene that still qualifies as original participation with Nature. Only in this case, the King of kings, Jesus, is confronting the self-proclaimed king of the fallen angelic order. It is the image of God reminding a wayward part of the temple that the story isn't over.

So, what really fell in the Fall? Like a mirror cracking, the condition of mankind changed, and suddenly the spirits in the temple who wanted to take advantage of the situation were the most powerful forces imaginable. Instead of a reciprocal relationship with Creation, Nature (as a whole, seen by a now-nervous, even diminished humanity) was now the dominant force, and we were often left helpless in its shadow. We traded our origins as the representation of God in the Cosmos for that of a lesser priest who needed to attend to these new "gods" ruling the Universe.

It gets worse. In calling Zeus "god," mankind was saying that it was in that spirit's image we were created. And for thousands and thousands of years, humanity believed that the sun and stars, the wind and waves, and the forests and mountains were the actual forces in control of life. Humans were the peasant subjects now in this story, not the co-rulers of the temple.

Our pagan ancestors had big problems, but seeing a spirit personifying the storm wasn't one of them. We often think that Jesus came to rid the world of paganism – and He did, just not in the way we most often think. Jesus came to restore our identity and fix the problem of the cracked mirror image brought about by the Fall. He came to take away the worship of spirit beings in Nature, but He clearly doesn't contradict their existence. Jesus's message was to follow *Him* and be restored, so that one day we could then free the Creation that has been waiting this entire time for the sons of God to be revealed.

| 13 |

The Scientific Revolution

Remember the amnesiac? Well, we've arrived now at the accident that stole our memories. It's called the Scientific Revolution, and if you've never heard of it before or given it much thought, I invite you to pay careful attention here. This upheaval changed the way we interact with Nature so drastically, that it's practically erased our memory of original participation. What it didn't erase of original participation, it set out to call "myth," "fantasy," "superstition," and "animism." A collective case of amnesia may be the only explanation of why we don't talk about this shift every morning at the breakfast table. It altered life that much.

For anyone reading this book and desiring to know what the future holds for our place in the Cosmic Temple, this is the moment we must understand; for if you can grasp this issue, you can answer Eustace's question about the nature of a star. To understand the Scientific Revolution is to possess the key to understanding our modern age, where we've come from, and what needs to happen from here. Some historians have even called this the biggest shift in human consciousness since the advent of Jesus Christ. Here's how it happened …

Imagine going all the way back to an early civilization, when the only kind of participation with Nature is what we have been calling "original." That's the kind where the varied parts of Creation are personified and represented by spiritual beings. We've also seen that most of original participation was marred by all the spirits who fell from their holy stature and were happy to be worshiped as gods and to deceive.

Now, if you're living back then, you are likely very interested in what those gods and goddesses are doing. In order to understand their moods, will, or character, you would look to the representations in Nature all around you that were linked to each particular spirit. Knowing the will of the gods was knowing what was going to happen in the Universe. That would have felt important.

Let's take the sun and the moon for our example. If an early culture believed that the sun and moon were just the physical representations of a sun or moon god (original participation), then they would be very interested in what the sun and moon were doing in their course through the heavens. They would want to know the sun's position in the sky, the exact phases of the moon, and perhaps, more ominously, when would the sun and moon overlap in an eclipse.

The behaviors of these *seen* objects were the signs and markers early cultures used to predict the behavior of the *unseen* spiritual beings. Therefore, knowing how to predict the behavior of the objects of Nature was a primary way to predict the behavior (or mood, if you will) of the gods.

Eclipses are good examples here because they were often interpreted as an ominous sign. If the sun (admittedly a very important part of life) suddenly went dark, then an original participant might infer that the gods and goddesses in the sun and the moon were up to something and needed to be appeased, or at least consulted. So, imagine in one of the early cultures the amount of work and study dedicated to predicting an eclipse! This required vast amounts of observation and theorizing.

In general, the motion of the heavenly bodies was one of mankind's first areas of interest. It was a good place to start because it's repetitive and cyclical. That predictable motion of the sun, moon, and planets made them easy objects of study, and since they were already high above our terrestrial, earthly life, they had a firm place in our minds as markers of the behavior of the gods. Therefore, figuring out those lights in the sky might have seemed like the most direct path to understanding the gods.

Years and years of observations would often lead to a working model of how the heavenly bodies moved around. Often, a physical model would have been made using circles and gears to accurately predict heavenly motion. If it worked and made accurate predictions, it was accepted as a good model. And as observations and experience grew, so too, did the quality of the models. Some of those early attempts were quite innovative, including a sun-centered model of the solar system postulated in ancient Greece around 500 B.C., a full 2,000 years or so before Galileo and his own sun-centered diagrams.

In the late 1500's and into the 1600's A.D (Galileo's timeframe) we can see the big shift happening. In a nutshell, we got better at math. I'm not kidding – if you really want to know what caused the Scientific Revolution, it's math. You are either laughing or crying right now, based on your own experience with this loved/hated subject. Like it or not, math is a kind of language, and it's a language that excels at describing the objective reality of things. Or we could say that it's good at describing the world if the outward, non-spiritual world was all there was to know. What it can't do is describe a spiritual, subjective experience (however, poetry does that job well).

Naturally, early scientists turned their new math skills to the one thing that we've sought to understand for ages – the motion of the heavenly bodies. It took a lot of work from astronomers like Galileo, Kepler, and Copernicus, along with the math skills of Isaac Newton, and in the end, there was a precise model of the solar system explaining the motions of the sun, moon, and planets. For the most part, that sun-centered model with elliptical (not a perfect circle) orbits has gone unchanged until the present day. But the important part here is that this is the first time we created a model that accurately explained the motions of the heavens. All the others fell short in one area or another. This was the first time it seemed we had cracked the code.

There's a lot of history to cover here, and we would be forgiven for feeling bogged down with this history-of-science lecture. Bear with it a moment longer. When you understand the beginning of science, you can unlock the mystery of why we see the world completely differently than our ancestors. Remember, this one change in thought altered the course of 95% of all of recorded human history. If you're like me, you want to know why.

| 14 |

Creating a New Truth

I think we can condense this drastic shift in consciousness into the following statement: we looked at the seemingly unerring model of the heavens and concluded that if the model can predict the nature and motion of the heavenly bodies without error, then the model is all the truth there is to know. That's it. That was the watershed moment. Prior to this, if a model predicted the behavior of the sun and moon (at least some of the time), then the model was useful, but was never believed to be the truth. That's because every observer before this moment knew the world was made up of natural, outward things that were connected to supernatural, unseen things (spirits).

Perhaps the lack of a super-accurate model helped that notion to go unchallenged, or maybe it wouldn't have mattered to someone thousands of years before anyway. We'll never know. What can't be argued is that before the Scientific Revolution, the "truth" of Nature could never be summed up in a knowledge of just the outward things. The truth could only be discerned by understanding the spiritual reality governing it all. The outward parts of Creation, like the sun and moon, were there to point toward the source of reality and truth on a higher plane.

The Scientific Revolution brought an end to this way of thinking, which is present in all of human history up until this moment in time.

This is worth repeating: all of the thousands of years of human experience until about 1600 A.D. were lived by people who took the spiritual component of Nature for granted. But with the development of a mathematically super-accurate model of the solar system, the nature of "truth" finally came into question. From this point on, the math and the science of the outward objects became the end of accepted human knowledge. I'll sum it up one last time in the statement:

> If you can explain the behavior of the outward objects without error, then the outward objects are all there is to know. There is no spiritual reality within Nature to understand.

An immediate effect of this was the denial of those spiritual beings that our ancestors thought were responsible for the behavior of Nature. You can see how this would work: once we found an equation that predicted the heavenly orbits, we suddenly felt empowered to explain everything that way. And our newfound predictive equations slowly turned our focus away from all those unseen, spiritual things that are so hard to understand and towards the concrete, objectified world that could be calculated into submission. By the time mankind had fully made this turn, we had convinced ourselves that we'd peered behind the spiritual curtain and found… math.

Let's appreciate this shift in our development with a keen eye. With each scientific step we took, we became more and more interested in a world that, for the first time, seemed like we could control. The line between "predict with math" and "control" is very thin. And with that newfound power came a distance between us and the spiritual reality of our ancestors. In a very short time, historically speaking, we arrived at the modern worldview: that the objects of Nature are now the *end* of the truth, instead of a midpoint between mankind and the spiritual beings created by God.

No longer was the sun a meeting place between mankind and a sun-like spiritual being. Now, the sun – just the physical object made up of hydrogen and helium gasses – was all the truth there was to know.

It effectively makes the objects around us *the* absolute truth. If we're going to deny the existence of a spiritual reality in Nature, the material stuff around us is all that's left. The physical material becomes the endpoint, instead of the representation, or at least the suggestion, of something else. If this feels like a strange form of idolatry to you, as if mankind just replaced the gods and goddesses of antiquity with the equations of science, then you might be on to something.

This shift in the 1600s was the first moment mankind had a reason to discount the spiritual intuition of our ancestors. For ages, all mankind had was an internal, spiritual sense of why an eclipse occurred. Now, mankind had mathematical formulas that could predict every eclipse, explain planetary orbits, and even calculate the power of the forces holding all the planets *in* their orbits. There had never been a culture that even came close to this kind of predictive power.

The amount of power that math and science put into our hands is staggering. To an early scientist, I'm sure it felt like they had peered behind the veil and, finding only mathematical equations, no longer needed spiritual beings to explain anything. They had a formula! I think those first, modern scientists can be forgiven for thinking they had discovered the absolute truth.

| 15 |

The Cosmic Machine

So where did that take us? Once the idea took hold – that there is only a physical reality with no spiritual beings inhabiting the aspects of Nature – mankind had the freedom to reimagine the nature of the entire Cosmic Temple. Only now, it won't be a temple anymore, because a temple is a place for spiritual activity and participation. If the Universe doesn't have a spiritual component, then it can only be seen as a self-regulating machine. Instead of spiritual personalities, we are left with simple inputs and outputs from predictive processes.

Think about how we look at trees today. Our educated minds see photosynthesizing leaves, bark and stems made of cellulose, and roots growing into a soil that is a composite of chemical elements. We don't see spiritual personality anymore because we have all grown up with the Scientific Revolution's version of faith: that the material make-up of the tree is all the truth there is to know.

All our modern lives are founded on this worldview, whether we like it or not. We were born into it, and you could say we take this for granted. In fact, almost everyone I know makes the same mistake of thinking that the way we see the world today is roughly the same way our ancestors did, yet nothing could be further from the truth. And when you consider how quickly our minds have been collectively rearranged on this issue, it's a bit staggering. Consider that the way we see the world would have been considered strange, foolish, or just plain prideful five or six hundred years ago.

Only five or six hundred years. That's a short period of time to handle such a drastic change, and we might expect to see equally drastic shifts in the everyday life of a human being on planet Earth because of it. And we do, starting with the incredible acceleration of development, industry, and technology. Using just the example of how we travel, we can see that the metaphorical foot was placed on the gas pedal in a way we had never experienced.

Did you know that until the Scientific Revolution, the fastest way to get about on land was the trusty old horse? This wonderful creature enjoyed the human travel speed record since the dawn of time. Then came along the steam engine in the 1800's, and the "iron horse" took over as the new fastest way to get about.

Now here's the crazy part. It took 5,600 years or so of history to go faster than the horse, but it only took another 150 years to send objects into orbit! We went from a horse's gallop to rocket power in the blink of an eye. I'm surprised our collective human consciousness doesn't suffer from whiplash! And this is just one development that took place faster than the human mind could contemplate what was even happening.

Factories, trains, airplanes, global economies, mass-produced food and clothing, computers, nuclear power, satellites, cell phones, and space exploration all came into our world at the same breakneck pace. Maybe we take for granted how much happened in just three or four centuries. We also might take for granted what it cost us.

In order to accomplish this feat, we needed to give ourselves the permission to exploit the resources of Creation at an unprecedented pace. I'm not suggesting that early humans didn't exploit the natural resources all around them (in as much as their limited technology allowed them to), but I believe their notions of a spiritual life within Nature put limitations on how much they took from the world. At the very least, you could say it slowed them down, since they had to consider another non-human presence in what they wished to use. Remember, our ancestors placed as much importance on spiritual knowledge as they did the dashboard knowledge that would allow them to advance through technology. That divided attention might be one reason why these industrial leaps weren't taken until our attention was only on the objective, physical reality. Whether this was a conscious or unconscious choice is a great question.

What we can say for certain is that our newfound power to exploit Nature – at will and in unprecedented, impactful ways – happened at the exact same time we stopped believing Nature had a voice to object to our actions.

I believe unapologetic exploitation in any relationship – human to human, human to animal, and human to environment – will always have negative results. Industrial working conditions, pollution, and habitat loss are all easy to see, but some other more personal consequences are starting to come to light. The invasion of electronic tech in our daily lives, at first a welcomed convenience, seems to be having a negative impact on our basic humanity, with studies already marking its negative effects on mental and physical health.

It's a good thing the Scientific Revolution was just a step in our development and not the final chapter! For now, we at least need to see the effects of forfeiting our awareness of a spiritual Nature. After all, it takes a human mind seeing the Cosmos as a lifeless, spiritless machine, made with gears, levers, and objectified nuts and bolts, to then create the modern working condition we know as a factory. It takes a denial of spiritual presence in the woods to feel like we can freely cut down an entire forest. It takes a mind with no consideration of personality in the waters to then pollute them for profit and convenience.

I'll leave you here with a poem from William Blake. You'll hear his perception of how the Scientific Revolution was changing life as we know it. You'll see his longing for a restored participation with Nature. And you'll see what he thinks about the industrialization of the world when he speaks of the "dark, Satanic Mills."

And did those feet in ancient time
Walk upon England's mountains green:
And was the holy Lamb of God,
On England's pleasant pastures seen!
And did the Countenance Divine,
Shine forth upon our clouded hills?
And was Jerusalem builded here,
Among these dark Satanic Mills?
Bring me my Bow of burning gold:
Bring me my arrows of desire:
Bring me my Spear: O clouds unfold!
Bring me my Chariot of fire!
I will not cease from Mental Fight,
Nor shall my sword sleep in my hand:
Till we have built Jerusalem,
In England's green & pleasant Land.

| 16 |

Nothing Left but Us

On the surface, this all seems very negative, but we cannot look at any of these developmental steps in only one dimension. The Scientific Revolution was as much a part of our story, the story that God has written for us, as was the original participation that preceded it. Yes, it came with very negative consequences, but so did the paganism of our ancestors. In each epoch of time, we see a hard-won development of the human being, steadily moving towards a final participation first described in Romans, chapter 8.

So, what did we gain from this stage of the journey? A blank slate. With our original ideas of fallen spiritual beings removed from our minds, we gained a world that was free from all original participation. As we've discussed, much of that falls into paganism, and ridding the world of that is a good thing.

With no spiritual beings on the other side of a spiritual veil of which we are conscious, we have an opportunity to start all over again, like a painter with a fresh new canvas. But there are a few more gains worth mentioning, even if they're a bit more subtle. For one, our ancestors could never have written a book like this about participation with the Cosmos simply because they took that participation for granted. They never *thought* about it the way we can now because it had always been instinctual. Think about anything we might call an instinct. Isn't it true that we take these things for granted?

When we say that someone "takes it for granted," we mean that they never give a thought about it *not* being there. We take for granted things that have never been absent from us. An instinct is in this category, which is why we can say our ancestors participated with Creation instinctually. When an instinct is suddenly absent, we have the power of comparison. We can compare having it as a "given" versus not having it at all. That power of comparison is what gives us the language to describe what it is we were taking for granted. In other words, we can talk about it, think about it, even reminisce about it, for the first time.

We are able to see it from the outside looking in, instead of right in the middle of it, where we never really knew what we had. So, falling *away* from a sense of participation with Nature actually gave us a description of what participation with Nature really is! We could rightly say that the Scientific Revolution gave us an actual mental understanding of what our ancestors instinctually experienced. These are equally important sides of the same coin.

The Scientific Revolution also changed our perceived role in the Cosmos as well. Think back to original participation. It *happened* to our ancestors; they really didn't have a say in the matter. Recall all of the myths and stories we've covered so far; the common denominator is that Nature was in control. The personifying spirits were the ones with all the power, and mankind was left to acknowledge their supremacy, often by worshipping those fallen spirits.

The Scientific Revolution removed those beings from our thoughts, and we were all that was left. That put us in charge of the world. We are the only ones who *could* be in charge in a post-Scientific Revolution world. Far from being a bad thing, this newfound sense of control in the world helped us to realize an important part of our humanity: freedom. The work of Jesus Christ and His famous words about bringing "freedom to the captives" continued to play out in our last 400 years, perhaps in a final way as we divorced our pagan origins.

To really understand our place in the Cosmos as "kings and priests" we had to first come face to face with a world that we are supposed to govern. You could certainly make an argument that our first steps into this role were filled with failure (and I would agree), but what child doesn't make mistakes? It is where we go from here that really matters.

Lastly, there is one more post-Scientific Revolution trend worth mentioning: individualism. Take a quick look at the last 400 years and you'll find humankind discovering a sense of self that was foreign to our predecessors. Our internal identity of an individual soul, capable of finding our way – completely separate from our surroundings – is a direct result of blocking out the voices in those "surroundings."

Someone living 1,000 years ago believed (again, in way they would have taken for granted) that the course of their life was at least influenced by those unseen forces in Creation. And in many cases, I'm sure they felt controlled by them. When we abandoned those influences, the only thing left to determine anything was ourselves. Cutting off the world of spiritual beings turned the focus of everything – all causes and effects – on just our individual souls. It's not a coincidence that tiny, individual atoms were discovered at the same time we discovered our individual selves.

I think this discovery, that every single person is alive and free *on their own* was well worth the wait. It gave us the perfect starting point to pioneer a new way of interacting with Creation. We'll dive into that in just a minute; but for now, just ponder the whole of the human experience. We've been on a 6,000-year odyssey to rediscover what we had a glimpse of in those first chapters of Genesis. This most recent step that gave us an experience of life without any spiritual essence in the world was just as important a step as a life that took it for granted.

Ralph Waldo Emerson, one of those rebel philosopher poets, wrote about how we might take something for granted, and what it might be like to rediscover its importance. Here is a passage he penned in his *Nature* essay:

> *If the stars should appear one night in a thousand years, how would men believe and adore; and preserve for many generations the remembrance of the city of God which had been shown! But every night come out these envoys of beauty, and light the universe with their admonishing smile.*

| 17 |

Adolescence, Adulthood, and Resurrection

Watching Man's relationship with Nature change over the millennia is a bit like seeing a pendulum swing back and forth. So much time was spent with Nature itself being the highest power, that when humans realized that they could be the masters, they went after it with gusto. Take a look at this statement from Owen Barfield, in which he summarizes the ideas of a forerunner of the Scientific Revolution, Francis Bacon:

> *Not only did he maintain that knowledge was to be valued for the power it gives man over nature; but he practically made success in this aim a part of his definition of knowledge.*

I've said earlier that it's best not to think of these forms of participation as right or wrong. They were each necessary for their time, and they each revealed something new about us and our role in the Cosmos. Developmentally, I'm not sure we've had much of a choice about these processes. They were/are inevitable. But the real question is, now that we've seen the two extremes of the pendulum swing, what can we do with all this understanding? What can we do about our relationship with Nature if we are able to choose something new, having experienced both imperfect extremes? Perhaps another metaphor might bring us a step closer to those answers.

Let's think about our role in the Cosmos using the familiar experience of growing up from childhood to adulthood. Do you remember your early years? Even if you don't, you've observed them in children around you. For an infant or toddler, life happens *to* you. You really don't have a say in the matter. When you eat, where you go, these are all determined by your parents. You are carried along (quite literally) by your overseers, and your effect on the world is passive and minimal.

The forces carrying you along are absolutely in charge. You owe your own well-being to them. In those early years you have a sense of those caretakers (mom and dad), and hopefully you feel love and affection from them. But you don't really understand them well, certainly not in the complex ways another adult would. Furthermore, you don't know a world without these grown-ups' influence, so you would take that for granted, not having anything different to compare it to. Does this sound familiar? It's a lot like original participation, after the Fall of Mankind.

What comes next, developmentally speaking, is adolescence. This phase of life is famous for its moments of willful independence, but what is going on underneath the classic teenage rebellion is a search for personal identity, away from outer influences. Adolescents want to find their own way and their own purpose as they take steps to be in charge of their own lives. They feel the need to separate themselves from their original caretakers, because no self-discovery can ever truly take place when someone is still managing your affairs. This willful, independent separation from an original state looks a lot like our years since the Scientific Revolution. And the discovery of self that pervades both adolescence and the last 400 years is no coincidence.

Then comes that moment of true adulthood, when you realize you no longer have to rebel in order to know who you are. You no longer have to pull away to feel independent. You can enter the world with purpose *and* self-knowledge. In life, this normally coincides with an acceptance and appreciation of your upbringing, along with a willingness to co-labor again.

The place of grown-up balance is a good way to begin talking about a final participation with Creation. Whatever happens from here, it can't be a return to the way it was. The way forward is never backward, and I can't imagine it was God's plan to return us to our infancy. We must grow up and inherit something for which we've finally come of age.

Could there be an even larger life metaphor for humanity in the Scientific Revolution? To find out, let's first ask the question, "What happens when you take the spirit out of something?" Most people would call that death, even if they're steeped in science. Now consider that we have done just that with the world around us. We have removed the spirit from Creation, and that left us with a dead environment. Just contrast the world of early Man, in which Nature was alive with voice and personality, with the world of today. Now, we know how to calculate and control Nature. We know how to define all its parts. But all that came at the expense of its inherent life (and spirit).

We didn't stop with our environment, either. After science took center stage, we began to think of ourselves as non-spiritual as well. We came up with explanations for everything, even our moods, that were in keeping with our inanimate, nuts-and-bolts view of the Universe. It's all brain chemicals and physical processes now, as if we're just smaller machines in a much larger cosmic machine. When pressed, science will admit to seeing humans as bags of chemicals, walking around in obedience to physical laws.

All of this brings us back to the metaphor. Could it be that the removal of spirit from our lives counts as a metaphorical death for humanity? Is it possible that we voluntarily walked ourselves into a tomb some 400 years ago? If this is an accurate picture, then it should give us new hope: there is always a death before a resurrection!

This death-to-resurrection theme is central to the gospel of Jesus Christ, and it might be playing out in our lives in more than one way. Maybe we are at the moment right before the stone is rolled away, and humanity is about to leave the tomb of a spiritless, dead world, and enter into a brand-new era of creation.

| 18 |

Intentional Participation

It bears repeating that the way forward is never backwards. You might feel that I favor the original participation of our ancestors, and that I'm a little harsh on our modern, scientific worldview, but it's only partly true. I'll admit that I wish we'd never left our original, spiritual understanding behind. But I wouldn't go back, even if given the chance.

No. The way forward is forward, and there's no sense wanting to go back to a state of infancy. And in truth, it would be impossible. We can't unlearn what science has given us. And if we did, we'd be forced to go through this whole process again and again until we arrived at the new kind of participation with Nature that God has intended for us all along. That new way of existence is the focus of this entire book.

It might help to define it first by what it is not. This is not a return to paganism, either in its ancient form or in the more modern, new age version where spirit-helpers are blindly followed without regard to their source. This must be absolutely clear if we're going to get this right. There's no room in this for fallen angelic beings masquerading as gods (or spirit guides), even though it is a return to a spiritual presence in the Cosmic Temple.

In this last step, the holy spiritual beings that have been faithfully serving God's kingdom are freed to inhabit Creation again. It's a picture of beautiful, holy objects in Nature being inhabited by the beautiful, holy spiritual beings God originally assigned to them. It would seem like a recreation of the Cosmic Temple. Or maybe it's an entry into the promised Sabbath rest, as if the work of Creation is finally done and it can simply exist as it was always meant to.

But we must remember that this step is a conscious choice. A new participation with Nature won't happen to us without our knowing about it. It involves a conscious decision to open our eyes anew to the world of the spiritual beings. And, with our newfound freedom of will, we can finally choose who it is we want to see.

Gone are the days of being at the mercy of fallen spiritual beings. And gone are the days of mistaking them for gods to be worshiped or followed. In this final step, it is the human who determines how the Cosmos is personified. After all, those rebellious, fallen angels posing as the gods of antiquity make up just a fraction of all the spiritual beings God created. They are the minority. There are far more that didn't fall from God's presence than those that did. Now it's time to get reacquainted with the majority – the holy spirit beings who have been waiting for us to come into our own.

That's why this last step could be called "Intentional." It will take a conscious choice on our part to meld together the spiritual perception of our ancestors with the freedom and Christ-likeness available to us today. And it's our choice to fill the world around us with a spiritual capacity that is for us, not against us. As I've mentioned before, original participation was something our ancestors took for granted. They never knew there was anything else. Should we decide to look again at the spiritual forces supplying the inner life of the Cosmic Temple, it will be a conscious act. A *choice*. And it will be all the more meaningful to us because we chose it over our current state.

More meaning isn't just a nice consolation prize for going through this whole journey. It is an amplifier for our future restoration of Nature. The meaning, the journey, and the intentionality of it all will make a connection with the Cosmos more powerful than anything that came before it. We may be returning to some lost spiritual understandings, but they'll get an upgrade the second time around.

Let's paint a picture of what this might look like. Imagine seeing the world around you with all its comprehendible glory. Imagine seeing the stars and the clouds and the trees and realizing, as only a modern human can, that those things are explainable and already well-known. Now, imagine inviting a holy, Christ-serving spiritual presence back into that scene. Perhaps they've been there all along just waiting for your perceptions to acknowledge them. Imagine visualizing a holy entity who inhabits and influences those stars, or clouds, or trees, as God intended and assigned. Think about the quality of relationship you could have with those parts of Nature once there is a holy and trustworthy voice and personality with whom you could connect.

It's as if we've made all the mistakes we can with Nature (we've certainly experienced the extremes) and we can finally bring forth the relationship only a mature son or daughter of God could. It is a perfect melding of everything we've learned in this human journey into a final, holistic, and intentional participation with the Cosmic Temple.

> *I consider that the sufferings of this present time are not worth comparing with the glory about to be revealed to us. For the creation waits with eager longing for the revealing of the children of God; for the creation was subjected to futility, not of its own will but by the will of the one who subjected it, in hope that the creation itself will be set free from its bondage to decay and will obtain the freedom of the glory of the children of God. We know that the whole creation has been groaning in labor pains until now...*
>
> *– Romans 8: 18 -22*

I wanted to give you the "freeing Creation" passage in its entirety, and I would recommend not passing over it too quickly. There are so many things connected in those versus: the significance of our mortal journey, the desire of Creation to be free, and the relationship between our own restoration and that of Creation. There's no doubt when you read Paul's statement that we're all locked together in this end-of-the-story fulfillment.

I'm hoping that will give you an appreciation for what we're talking about here in this book. We're the first humans in history who have the opportunity to relieve the futility and bondage that has been the human/Creation condition for our entire mortal story. In some Bible translations, the word "futility" is rendered "frustration," and I think that does a good job of giving voice to what we've all been through throughout these thousands of years.

All the futility and frustration that Creation has endured can be summed up in the two forms of misunderstanding we've been diagraming in the previous chapters. There's the idolatry of paganism. And there's the more subtle idolatry of the Scientific Revolution, when we mistakenly called the objects (or the objectifying) of Nature the absolute truth, making them into false gods once again.

In both stages of the journey, we've been missing what Creation really is. It isn't our gods or our God, and it isn't a lifeless, objectified machine. It's the Cosmic Temple, and it is eagerly awaiting the day when we will cast off *all* of our idolatry. Can you imagine how excited all of Nature must be to behold a mature humanity who is ready to take our place as God's representative in the Universe?

| 19 |

The End of the Journey

You've made it to the end of this historical tour of Man and Nature, and perhaps now we have a nice overview of the changing way we see our world. Additionally, I hope we've got a firmer grasp on the collective amnesia of which we've all partaken. It was a trade, so to speak, between the knowledge (or memory) of our ancestors and the knowledge gained through science. It was, after all, self-induced amnesia. Think for a moment of those times when you were learning something entirely new, but then had trouble recalling something you knew before. Aren't we all familiar with that feeling of having the old information pushed out to make way for the new?

On the grandest of scales, we've consumed and internalized so much information in just the last few hundred years that the previous knowledge of how the world works – on another plane – was simply pushed out in favor of the new and powerful objective details. We traded in the original, spiritual design of the Cosmos, in order to gain air travel, modern medicine, computers, and internet-provided streaming media content.

The man on the street probably doesn't have an appreciation of the magnitude of information that he is bombarded with every day, often even before breakfast, in comparison with his distant ancestor. What is considered common knowledge about the human body, global politics, the weather, and who is doing what in the lives of celebrities is a level of detailed information that no one, in the history of man, has ever tried to comprehend. And often we are acutely aware of things thousands of miles away, as if the information of the entire globe is information that pertains to our own individual, everyday lives.

Again, I'm not arguing here that the hard-won information boom of science isn't good or helpful, just that it was impossible to keep enough room for both worlds in our minds. Something had to be "forgotten."

And now, some 400 years into our scientific existence, we've discarded our spiritual past so thoroughly that to some, taking the time to consider what's happened to humanity throughout history would be considered a colossal waste – maybe even something that would be impossible to do. There's at least no denying that life is busier and faster-paced in our modern world. Who has time to stop and think about what came before this? Who has time to even stop and think? To stop. To think. Those are things we don't emphasize in our current global culture where it seems your value as a human lies in your acceptance and consumption of the constant onslaught of distractions.

So stop, think, and take a moment to congratulate yourself. You've managed to stick with this journey through our history despite our modern tendencies to avoid this kind of investigation. Any effort to go forward from here will be, by default, counter-cultural, so get used to the notion of doing something that goes against the acceleration of the modern world.

That brings me to one last metaphor, and this one comes straight from Owen Barfield. At the very beginning of his book, *Poetic Diction,* he came up with a simple picture that expresses not just what we've been though on this journey, but also what might be just up ahead. I'll give you my best paraphrase of what he wrote, mixed with some of my own embellishments...

Imagine the entire Universe is a car, and in this car, there are front seat and back seat passengers. The ones sitting up front (where all the controls are) are interested in the question, "How can we work it?" The passengers in the back seat are asking the subtly different question,

"How does it work? Those two questions (and the passengers asking them) are looking for different kinds of information.

The front seat folks want to know how to work the car – or how to make the car work for them. We could say they want to *control* it. They're looking for the surface knowledge that will help them get the results they want (think back to "dashboard knowledge"). Fundamentally, they want to direct its capabilities to further their goals.

The back seat passengers want to know how the car works. They want to know what unseen mechanisms cause it to move. Because they can't get out of the car to look at it, they have to trust their internal senses about what kind of engine makes it go and on what kind of road it could travel. They want to know the car, itself, so that they can better understand its purpose, and by association, their own purpose as well. In the back seat, it's believed that by knowing how the car works, a passenger might one day be able to influence it *as it was designed,* not necessarily in whatever direction seemed good to the occupant simply because it was possible.

I think anyone would agree that both sets of passengers are important, but that's not how the human story goes. As the front seat people figured out all the levers and buttons, they pressed forward in their attempt to work (or control) the car. They became increasingly dismissive of the back seat passengers who seemed to look to their inward senses and a deeper, more spiritual observation of the vehicle for truth.

Eventually, something like a divider was put up between the two groups, with the front seat passengers declaring that their kind of knowledge (the kind that increases our ability to make the car – or Creation – do what we want) was the only kind that mattered. As you know, that argument won the day a few hundred years ago during the Scientific Revolution, and the front seat group has been leading the way (and dismissing the backseat group) ever since. The back seat group just wasn't willing to jettison an active understanding of the car, itself, simply so that we could "get somewhere" more quickly.

Now, the front seat group was great at finding all the buttons, levers, and controls on the car. When they found one, they would push, pull, and press until they learned how to use it. Soon, they had found all the obvious ones, so they went looking for smaller and smaller levers and controls to manipulate. They even created controls to do what they wanted. What they didn't realize is that no matter what control they touched or created, the net result was always acceleration.

Let's take a parenthetical detour here to make sure we get Barfield's metaphor. He was accurately pointing out that once science had figured out the mechanics of our world on the large (macro) scale, it started looking at smaller and smaller aspects of the Cosmos, even past the tiniest scale (micro) all the way to the subatomic. And, when you look back at this journey, it's true that as we found smaller and smaller "levers and buttons," the pace of everything accelerated.

Interestingly, the "smaller" we've explored, the greater the acceleration of our development. That is one reason why it's so important to ponder the 5,000 or more years of horse-drawn motion and the rapid jump from the steam engine to rocket power in the blink of an eye.

Barfield ended his metaphor with a warning; for in his story, the car simply did not go on accelerating forever. It crashed. That's what any car will do if you step on the accelerator pedal and don't let up no matter what. You're going to run into something eventually, and Barfield imagined that we all might want to hear from the back seat passengers again after we've wrecked the car.

| 20 |

The End or the Transition?

Let's talk about that crash for a moment. I believe we're nearing the end of an age as we speak. I think that's true from both an astronomical and a historical perspective. My previous book *Cosmic Shift* was written about this issue, and the conclusions I made there go something like this: there are cosmic (or astronomical) ages that are affirmed in the Biblical record and explain a great deal about the major shifts in the narrative of God and Man. The ages act like chapters in a story, and when those ages change, it opens up new understandings and practices, often in major, upheaving ways.

Based on history and astronomy, I concluded that we are in a transition between cosmic ages right now, and that means we should expect the same kinds of upheavals in many areas of life as one cosmic door closes and the next one opens up. Just a quick glance at the last shift, marked by the life of Jesus Christ, Himself, can show you how tumultuous these transitions can be. It's important to note here that a tumultuous time doesn't have to be the "end," but simply a transition into something new.

Try to remember that as we discuss a forthcoming crash. If you don't like that word, then maybe just call it an "arresting cosmic adjustment." Or, like my last book title, a "shift."

I can imagine such an adjustment occurring simply because there aren't any checks on our breakneck pace of technological development. We seem determined to push the envelope on everything, and there's no concern at all these days that we're using and exploiting things every day that we don't truly understand. We have tons of dashboard knowledge on how to use it, and a severe lack of motivation to *know* it.

It reminds me of the myth of Atlantis. According to some old writings, there was once a great civilization that came to an abrupt end. In our modern storytelling, we like to imagine Atlantis as an advanced culture that got prideful and was brought down by the very advancements that made it great. Fast-forward to our modern world for an eerie similarity. We've become totally dependent on technology we understand only superficially, and that dependence may create problems too big for us to solve. It's possible we're there already, considering our modern world pursues artificially intelligent systems like some sort of technological holy grail.

If the crash isn't caused by a technology that spins out of our control, then perhaps it's a crash of the human spirit itself. Or perhaps both occur at the same time. I, for one, feel it's plainly obvious that the more tech-dependent we become, the more our true humanity seems to disintegrate. I'm aware of the studies that track an increase in depression and anxiety with increased cell phone and social media use, but I'm talking about something bigger... and yet more subtle.

There seems to be (at least to me) a decline of critical thinking skills and reading comprehension, a lack of deep thought, and a decline of dialectic reasoning. We've become one-dimensional and un-nuanced. This simplifying (or dumbing-down) of the human being seems to coincide with the advent of our tech-driven life. Instead of the tech making us all smarter and more fully human, it's slowly reducing us to mere animals.

Perhaps on the most basic level, this kind of technology-driven and technology-dependent life is just not what God designed for us. And if He didn't, who did? Who is "winning" from this scenario? For the sake of contrast, consider the differences between our modern life, where every function is linked through technology to many other systems all over the world, with the natural simplicity of the verse:

> *but they shall all sit under their own vines and under their own fig trees, and no one shall make them afraid...*
>
> *– Micah 4: 4*

It's as if the life God imagined for us is categorically different from our globally dependent grocery stores, international banks, and endless layers of phone lines, power cords, computer wires, and digital signals. When I imagine sitting under my own vine and fig tree, I sense a sigh of relief. It feels like the promised Sabbath rest of Creation. It would be a place to ponder, observe, and understand. To participate.

That kind of life is the polar opposite of the endless pushing and corralling of the modern world, as if we're all in a cell phone maps app that directs the car where it wants it to go and never lets the vehicle stop. If the car needs to crash in order for us to find our own vine and fig tree, then it could be considered an act of mercy.

> *When the velocity of progress increases beyond a certain point, it becomes indistinguishable from crisis.*
>
> *– Owen Barfield*

| 21 |

Dominion or Domination?

We've got some ideas now of what this "arresting cosmic adjustment" might look like, but at the core of any scenario is our unchecked exploitation of Nature and our unwillingness to really know what it is we're even exploiting. Think back to the moment when unchecked exploitation became possible. It occurred right when we decided there wasn't anything to *know* in the Cosmic Temple anymore.

It marked the beginning of the unrestrained development that Barfield imagined as the car accelerating out of control. The wall that he imagined the car crashing into is a forced reckoning with our role in the Cosmos, and when we hit it, we'll have to ask the hard question: will we continue to use and exploit what we don't truly know, and sometimes don't even care about knowing or understanding? Or will we decide to have a participatory relationship with Creation itself? Will we be exploitative consumers and controllers, or true human kings?

The issue of our kingship is crucial to this final step, and it was designed into the human experience from the very beginning.

> *God blessed them, and God said to them, "Be fruitful and multiply, and fill the earth and subdue it;* ***and have dominion*** *over the fish of the sea*

> *and over the birds of the air and over every living thing that moves upon the earth."*
>
> *– Genesis 1: 28 (emphasis added)*

But what comes to mind when we think of rulers and kings? If you're like me, you go back to all the kings throughout history, and that can be depressing.

Human kingship hasn't looked good over the millennia, and it's a struggle to find a positive example. More often than not, kings look like greedy, petty bullies. So, do we really want to bring back kings and queens and royalty? Or is there something more fundamental about our comprehension of "ruling" that needs to change?

Now you might be thinking to yourself, "Yes, but if given the chance, Christopher, I'll be good at it. I'll be a noble, virtuous king unlike all those bullies from history." Not so fast, my friend. There may be more to our idea of kingship that needs to change aside from us just not being mean and greedy in our royal "dominion-ing." Maybe the whole idea of ruling needs an arresting cosmic adjustment too.

Think for a moment about a good, noble ruler. Even if we take out all the bad stuff, don't we still imagine a king as a person *in charge*? Don't we imagine them being *in control*? It's as if the primary function of a king is to exercise power; but this is where the true human king, Jesus the Christ, enters into the story and redefines for a longing Creation what it means to rule. For with Jesus, the primary function of a king is to *relate.*

Take a walk through the Gospels and you'll get to know a brand-new kind of kingship. Jesus, unlike any other human born into royal power (and His was immense, for sure), never forces anyone to obey Him. He might force a demonic spirit to release its hold on a human, and He might forcefully discipline some money changers in His temple, but He never forced a human being to accept His kingdom and His rule. He consistently allows a person to choose their own path.

Unlike a human king, He never calls on His vassals to come kiss His ring or pay homage to Him. He is, in almost every respect, a king without ceremony. He lacks the fanfare that says, "Look at me! I'm a king! Come bow down!" Even His triumphal entry into Jerusalem, which was the most fanfare He ever received, was subdued compared to most king-related entries. He did the whole procession riding on a donkey.

If He doesn't rule in the normal ways, then how does He do it? He rules through relationship. Just watch His interactions in the Gospel accounts as He spends time with people, healing their diseases and caring about their lives. He answers their tough questions and enters into life with them. He eats with them, travels with them, gives them comfort, and allows them access to His life. In three short years, He changed the entire notion of how a king actually rules. He took the classic picture of a ruler, seated high above his subjects in some ivory tower, and replaced it with friendship and mutual vulnerability.

I could simplify the whole idea this way: Jesus rules what He *knows*. He rules from a place of true relationship. That's the contrast. In our modern view of ruling, we think it's possible to have authority over something without any relational investment or mutual vulnerability. Now turn that on its head and you'll see the Jesus method of kingship: get to know the subject first; then out of that relationship, your position as a true king will be obvious.

As an aside, someone might want to make the case that Jesus' meekness was just one side to His character, and if He chose, He could appear as quite the stately king with a vast angelic army to back Him up. I think we can all agree that this is true, and that when the time comes for Him to reveal that aspect of His kingship, it will be magnificent. The important thing here is to see how He chose to express His power initially. It's these first foundations of kingship that I think we need to review.

With a relational kingship in mind, try to reimagine the moment Jesus walked on the waters. If you're following the worldview I've been setting up in this book, then you might re-think that story a little. It's not a picture of Jesus forcing lifeless, liquid water to somehow behave as a solid so He could walk across. Perhaps it's a picture of the author of Creation relating to a spiritual presence in the Sea of Galilee that He *knew.* Maybe Jesus had a relationship with the waters, and just like the humans who followed Him, those waters had already figured out who He was, and they would have carried Him anywhere.

Perhaps our biggest problem in the days ahead – the most arresting part of the crash – is our realization that dominion does not mean domination. I think that bears repeating, since the word "dominion" has been used to excuse some pretty wretched behaviors in history. *Dominion does not mean domination.*

A worldly king can dominate. Anyone, for that matter, can force something into submission with enough power. And certainly, this is the attitude we've taken with Nature. But to exercise true dominion, as we have been destined to release on the earth, we must rule the way Christ ruled, through an actual relationship.

We've got our work cut out for us as we seek a Christ-like connection with the spiritual personalities of Nature.

Part 2

The Role of Imagination

| 22 |

The Journey Within

There are words in our language that, if used in a certain context, can make us very uncomfortable. *Imagination* is one of them. Some think of it as make-believe and the distractions of childhood. For others, it's upheld as a noble part of the human spirit and a window into a world of creativity. To suggest that it can be a path to truth, though, can introduce the aforementioned uneasiness no matter where you stand.

But we can't shy away from it. We've arrived at the point in this journey where we'll need some tools to get us practically involved in the business of freeing Creation, and that will demand we look into the potential power of our imaginations. And we need to know this word's connection to the "spiritual eyes" or "eyes of the heart" I mentioned in the introductory chapters.

This is, after all, a spiritual pursuit. And spiritual pursuits need spiritual perceptions to lead the way. We'll need to know (quite confidently I think) if imagination can do that job, since we typically think of it as just a tool for fictional stories rather than a way to actually "see" things. Let's allow the history and the development of the word itself to inform us…

As our ancestors changed the way they thought and interacted with their world, they also changed the way they used words. This is a well-documented part of history. As our thinking changes, so does our language. As an aside, this is an incredibly interesting subject to me as a writer. Charting the evolution of thinking with the evolution of literature is like discovering a mystery in human development!

Our word "imagination" has not arrived in these modern times without going through some language changes as well. Today, it's synonymous with "fantasy" or "make-believe," and that seems a far cry from a possible path to truth. The question we should be asking is, "Is that always what it has meant, or is there more to it? Let us harken back to an idea that precedes imagination. We can find it in the word (or idea of) "inspiration."

Inspiration is an old concept that the creative power of mankind comes from a source *outside of* mankind. The word itself gives us this picture. Inspiration means "in-spirit." To be inspired, in the original sense of the word, was to have a spirit (from outside of you) come to reside in you and cause some kind of creative spark or process. It's the old idea of a muse. To be inspired was to be *in-spirited* with a kind of divine creative force separate from yourself.

It's important to know here that when our ancestors felt like a human was working with powers or ideas from across the veil in that heavenly realm, they believed it was because some spirit from that realm entered and made it all possible. For fun, take some time to research the words "genie" and "genius" and you'll find the same ideas at work. The genie, or spirit, was what made the genius. Or search for the phrase "the Spirit of the Lord came upon..." in the Bible. In both cases you'll see the picture ancient humans had of the human connection to that divine creative force. There were spirits (or God's Spirit) outside of man that could come *inside* man for a time in order for some otherworldly experiences to occur.

So what's the big deal with thinking our divine moments are from an outside spirit? Well, like all things, it didn't stay that way forever. I bet you already know the Scientific Revolution plays a role here, because we saw how much the causes and effects of everything became internalized in the last centuries. With no spiritual beings in our consciousness, the only possible source of the creative spark is *within* us. But the roots of this change can be traced back far earlier than the Scientific Revolution, it just took some time to trickle down. To find it, look no further than the book of Acts, chapter 2.

> *When the day of Pentecost had come, they were all together in one place. And suddenly there came from heaven a noise like a violent rushing wind, and it filled the whole house where they were sitting. And there appeared to them tongues as of fire distributing themselves, and they rested on each one of them. And they were all filled with the Holy Spirit ...*
>
> *– Acts 2: 1-4 (NASB)*

The revealing of the Holy Spirit to mankind is a big deal for innumerable reasons. For this discussion, let's focus on how the Holy Spirit came upon each individual believer, and after this moment, the Spirit is said to dwell *in* us.

> *since the Spirit of God dwells in you...*
>
> *– Romans 8: 9*

The idea of God's Spirit coming into mankind is a bit like inspiration, but with one big difference – the Spirit that came inside us never left. Even more, the Spirit has a home in us (dwells in us). This broke the previous barriers of how that "divine creative force" from the heavenly realm could interact with us on a personal level. From here on, the divine creative force – the Holy Spirit – became a permanent part of humanity's metaphysical makeup.

Now, think about how thousands of years of inspiration had been turned on its head when the source of creative power came to dwell inside mankind – and remained there. What was once only outside of us was now a permanent part of us. It fundamentally changed what we are on the inside.

All right (you might be saying), so what if inspiration becomes internal? What does that have to do with imagination? I'm glad you asked. Once inspiration was placed inside of us, we needed new words to describe a personal force that could do those divinely creative wonders. Enter into our vocabulary the word "imagination." But let's not get too hasty. There are more steps worth mentioning before imagination fully took on the job of inspiration.

| 23 |

Open Your Eyes

Mankind knew of our ability to picture something outside of our immediate senses before the Holy Spirit's introduction in Acts, but we didn't really think about it until just a few hundred years before Christ (or at least we didn't write about it). Aristotle mentions this faculty as the word "phantasia," and the phrase "mind's eye" or "eyes of the mind" comes into use at about the same time in the Greco-Roman world.

This was the early development of our ideas about what happens inside a person when we envision things that aren't present to our outer senses. So, we can say that the faculty existed, but hadn't been explored. Or perhaps that faculty was simply in its infancy, waiting on the moment in the Upper Room when the Holy Spirit deposited a new source of creative power. It's important to note here that our ability to picture things in our minds was around before these moments, but it just wasn't talked about or thought about. It might help to understand how humans can possess a faculty but never really think about it by revisiting the ideas of original and final participation.

Original participation was, as you recall, an instinctual view of the Cosmos. It was a view of the world that everyone took for granted, and at its foundations it might have even been an unconscious participation. The final participation that we've discussed is intentional, and it's a very conscious choice. Think of our "mind's eye" that way too.

For most of history, it exists as something we just instinctually used, but never fully identified. To talk about it, on any level, means it has left that unconscious area and entered into the forefront of our minds where it can be dissected and appraised. Once you do that, it can't be put back in that former state where it's taken for granted. The process of bringing it into our conscious thought began in those centuries before Christ, as if we were building up to the moment when our internal, spiritual senses could be fully revealed, a process that is still at work today.

What we can say for sure is that because of the indwelling Spirit, our internal processes got the biggest jolt since God breathed life into Adam; and it would stand to reason that what we thought of as the "mind's eye" would get a serious empowerment as well. Not surprisingly, in the decades after the Holy Spirit's introduction, these internal eyes start to play a bigger role:

> *...with the eyes of your heart enlightened, you may know what is the hope to which he has called you, what are the riches of his glorious inheritance among the saints,...*
>
> *– Ephesians 1: 18*

> *...because we look not at what can be seen but at what cannot be seen, for what can be seen is temporary, but what cannot be seen is eternal.*
>
> *– 2 Corinthians 4: 18*

> *...they became enraged and ground their teeth at Stephen. But filled with the Holy Spirit, he gazed into heaven and saw the glory of God and Jesus standing at the right hand of God.*
>
> *– Acts 7: 54 -55*

Additionally, there's a new state of being called "in the Spirit" that takes center stage after the watershed moment in Acts 2. And when John is "in the Spirit" throughout the book of Revelation, he sees all sorts of heavenly things that were not present to his bodily senses. He was imprisoned on the island of Patmos, after all, so he was definitely paying attention to more than the jail cell that filled his point of view.

A good question at this point might be, "If they were talking about imagination, why didn't they just say that instead of that 'eyes of your heart' phrase?" Here is where we need an understanding of how words evolve over time. Our modern word "imagination" had yet to be invented. It took a Latin root (imaginari) to create that word, and that wasn't well documented until the last 700 years or so. The best the Apostle Paul had to work with while writing the letter to the Ephesians was the term he used: the "eyes of your heart."

We might take it for granted today, but the ideas of what made up the imagination actually were just being formed when the New Testament was written. This is just my personal opinion, but I think the Apostle Paul would have used the word "imagination" had it existed when he wrote his letters to the churches. It would make his introductory statement in Ephesians 1:18 read:

I pray... with your imagination enlightened, you may know...

Let's try to summarize this evolution of thought. In the ancient world, the Spirit of the Lord came *upon* someone for a time or for a task. In the book of Acts, the Spirit of the Lord came to dwell in us permanently – as a new part of ourselves. Therefore, we needed a way to talk about how we perceive this new place inside us that stayed connected to God. We needed words that could explain how we perceive divine things from within, instead of from without.

When a new idea is presented to a people, it is first explained not with brand-new words, but with pre-existing words that best describe it. Our ancestors reached for those phrases already circulating in our consciousness like "mind's eye" and "eyes of your heart." Hence, the new internalized and permanent inspiration was best talked about in terms of internal eyes that could see into that other spiritual, heavenly, divine world.

Those forerunner words eventually coalesced into what we think of as "imagination," the modern word that best describes our ability to perceive beyond our external senses. What is often lost on us is that whatever else our imaginations can be (daydreaming, flights of fancy, etc.), it was formed as the successor to inspiration. Even if just in part, our imaginations are designed as a constant connection to the Divine creative force.

But as you know, that isn't quite the end of the story. The Scientific Revolution got a hold of this word and did the work for which it is famous. It took the spirit right out of the word and relegated its uses to more nuts-and-bolts meanings. When scientific thinking is allowed to go to its extreme, it removes the other, heavenly world from everything and seeks only its measured, objectified answers and origins. So, when science became the only valid way to see Creation, imagination lost the meaning of "Divine creative force" and was only allowed to play in the minds of children as make-believe.

We've now seen the full evolution of the word from its original adoption as a way to talk of our newfound, internal inspiration to the modern, Latin-based term, and then to its common, post-scientific weakening. But a strange thing happened while this word was becoming less important to the scientific world. A group of people unwilling to be carried along with the tide refused to let go of the origins of our internal eyes. In fact, they dug in their heels and contended for the strength of imagination as a connection to spiritual truths.

They created the first comprehensive theories of imagination as they rebelled against the attitude of their scientific age. You could make the case that they explored imagination more thoroughly than anyone had before them. Amazing how a little opposition can cause something to grow and get stronger. If you hadn't guessed it already, these were the same rebels I mentioned in the early chapters – poets, philosophers, and theologians who held on to the wisdom of the past while the rest of the world was ready to call it all a delusion.

I've included at the end of this chapter some of my favorite quotes from these revolutionary thinkers. What I hope you get from perusing them is a newfound appreciation of how this word has taken a journey parallel to our own. And since daring to reimagine the word "imagination" is a tough task, you might want to refer to these quotes (and their authors) when you need a little encouragement to keep going. "Imagination" is a word with a rich history and a powerful purpose. Our discovery of its full strength has arrived at the perfect time. Perhaps now, on the cusp of restoration, is the moment it's needed most.

By the way, none of this is meant to diminish inspiration. It's still needed! Anyone who has tried to write a book and says otherwise is lying. But inspiration alone won't get the job done. We'll need our very personal, internal sense of creative power, which was given to us to do this very thing – to reimagine Creation. If you're following the thread here, reimagining something is the first step to re-creating it.

I rest not from my great task! To open the Eternal Worlds, to open the immortal Eyes, of Man inwards into the Worlds of Thought, into Eternity, ever expanding in the Bosom of God, the Human Imagination.

– Blake, Jerusalem 5: 18 -20

The primary imagination I hold to be the living power and prime agent of all human perception, and as a repetition in the finite mind of the eternal act of creation in the infinite I Am.

– Samuel Taylor Coleridge

I am certain of nothing but the holiness of the heart's affections, and the truth of imagination.

– John Keats

The imagination may be compared to Adam's dream. He awoke and found it truth.

– John Keats

A systematic approach towards final participation may therefore be expected to be an attempt to use imagination systematically.

– Owen Barfield

Iconoclasm is made possible by the seed of the Word stirring within us, as imagination.

– Owen Barfield

| 24 |

Trust and Results

Since imagination is taught as an ability to picture something in your mind (say, an airplane flying in the sky) and not as an ability to picture an accurate spiritual reality in your mind, (say, a spiritual being that gives voice to the waters), it's common to need some reassurance that we're doing something sane and fruitful. It's not like imagination theory and application are mainstream studies these days. So, let's try to warm up to the idea that it can be trusted as something more than just our wandering, picturing minds.

Let's start with this subtle distinction: we don't need to trust imagination itself, but rather a set of spiritual senses we've come to call imagination in our modern language. The spiritual senses responsible for internal, otherworldly perception have been brewing for millennia. The modern word we use to describe those senses has been around for far less time. At least for me, that helps make the mental leap, since I'm as much a product of the post-scientific world as anyone and had to see for myself that my imagination senses were a bridge to that unseen, heavenly world.

My first experience with this, as I've documented in other books and mentioned in the introductory chapters, was the single greatest revolution of my life. If you've never read my other accounts, I'll give you the briefest of versions: I walked into a prayer meeting focused on inner healing, and I walked out convinced I could participate with heaven. It was all so unexpected.

The Christian pastors I met with were prepared for the kind of prayer time where you ask God to reveal and help you deal with past hurts and insecurities. This kind of prayer utilized the imagination (without really calling it that) as you would often remember emotionally crippling events in your life and then picture Jesus there with you as you sorted it all out and healed. This is more or less how it happened with me, although I wasn't expecting my internal eyes to keep showing me things after I had worked through some unresolved issues. But they did, and the healing journey continued on as Jesus took me to God's throne and eventually to a door leading to a lush, green garden. I was stunned at the entrance to paradise, but even more so when the promise came from Jesus that I could "Come here and walk and talk with Me as often as you like."

As you would expect, I took the Lord up on the offer to visit the garden of paradise with Him as often as I liked. Who wouldn't take that deal? I went back every day, and I haven't stopped after all these years. It's important to note here that all of this occurred with those same internal eyes we've been talking about. I didn't know it was imagination then, but it was certainly the spiritual sense that was at work. I wasn't seeing anything with my biological eyes, and I wasn't out-of-body in any way. It was, without a doubt, an internal experience that elevated my consciousness to another plane – safely – since Jesus, Himself, was there.

Now, anyone paying attention to the otherworldly claims made in this story might ask why I put any faith in my experience. The answer is two-fold. I had long desired a quality of relationship with God that was never satisfied by the normal, status-quo, Christian life. To be where Jesus ascended in the heavenly realms and carry on a conversation as we walked around paradise was too good to pass up. All my spiritual senses were working, and I felt I was finally experiencing the closeness the New Testament promised in our relationship with God.

After this first meeting "in the Spirit," where I felt I was with Jesus in His current habitation in the heavenly realms, I was hooked. I've never gone back to my pre-eyes-of-my-heart understanding simply because I've loved the closeness to God. Being able to see the Lord and hear His voice, all with those imaginal senses, brought an element of realism that was missing in my former prayer life. Just ask yourself which would feel closer: a long-distance phone call with God or an actual walk around the garden in person?

The other reason I learned to trust these experiences was because of the results. Again, this is well-documented in my other books, and while I have no expectation that my word alone will be sufficient to convince you, I'll say it anyway. There were so many affirmations that my journeys "up there" in the Spirit were affecting the actual living of my mortal life here on earth. I learned that what I could see with the eyes of my heart was an actual reality. It could show me the truth. And, the effects of that truth ranged from miraculous healing to simple help and guidance as I lived out my life. In short, I was convinced because of the proof.

The need for proof is important, and no one should feel unbelieving for demanding it. On the most foundational level, interacting with the heavenly realms – no matter how you do it – should bear *good fruit.* The easiest way to identify that is with the fruit of the Holy Spirit named in the Bible: things like love, joy, peace, kindness, self-discipline, etc. Those Christ-like traits should be on the increase if our imaginal experiences are to be trusted, and if I hadn't seen those positive effects on my character or well-being, I would not still be doing this today. I can think of no better proof or test to affirm the use of imagination as a bridge to all of heaven's unseen things.

| 25 |

Get on the Bridge

A question I'm often asked is, "Was this always easy for you?" The short answer is "Yes" and "No." Yes, it was an easy journey. I never asked for this to happen, it just happened. In that way, my inaugural experience with the eyes of my heart was a lot like inspiration. It *came upon* me, without my foreknowledge or even consent. It was not a conscious act. And after that first experience, for at least a few weeks, it remained an effortless pursuit. I just didn't know any better, and I hadn't thought deeply about what was happening. I would simply open the eyes of my heart and ascend to that place where Christ is seated at the right hand of the Father.

But it didn't stay effortless forever. After that initial "honeymoon phase", I felt my new extra-sensory prayer life bogging down. It got harder and harder to believe what I was perceiving, or even to focus on anything with my internal eyes. Looking back, I'm actually very grateful for this minor inconvenience because, without it, I never would have connected what was happening to me with the "imagination" we've been talking about.

That understanding developed like this: when using the eyes of my heart started to become difficult, I initially thought it was because I lacked something. It was as if I had ridden out that initial wave of inspiration and once I started to think more about what was happening,

I mistakenly thought I would need more inspiration to keep going. Without realizing it, I was waiting for God to do something that God had already done.

Now, don't misunderstand this as an example of why we shouldn't think too much about the spiritual blessings we receive. I've heard it said all too often that in order to experience spiritual things, we'd have to shut out our intellect and just believe. I'll never deny that God does things we can't explain, but I think it's sheer foolishness not to pursue understanding. Wanting to have wisdom about a newfound spiritual pursuit is never the problem. Back to the story...

Once I realized that I was making all of this too hard, and all I needed to do was trust the spiritual faculty I had been given, as is, all the original effortlessness returned. Instead of waiting and worrying if heaven would open for me, I got used to using this free pass called imagination. And I got used to it being a conscious choice. In other words, the original inspiration opened the door, but intentional imagination is what has allowed me to walk through it as often as I'd like.

However, using imagination this way – this liberally – brings with it some new concerns we've not had to think through until now. One of which is this: I've been making the case so far that imagination is trustable, but you might recall that imagination can also be known as flights of fancy (or fantasy), and that doesn't sound like something in which we would want to put our faith. A flight of fancy, as the name suggests, is that *other* capacity of imagination to randomly daydream, recall a memory, etc. It's a useful mental tool, but a far cry from an accurate picture of the unseen world. This one glaring issue is what stops many people from using the imagination for any serious purpose.

I think the solution to this problem can best be explained with a metaphor. Let's consider imagination as a bridge. On one side of the bridge is fantasy. On the other side is the Divine creative force, or what we've been referring to as Holy Spirit-empowered spiritual senses. On the one side, the eyes of your heart can show you something silly, made up, remembered, or in the worst sense, false or evil. That's not an exhaustive list, just a basic idea of flights of fancy.

On the other side, the eyes of your heart could show you Jesus, God's throne room, the garden of Eden, or any heavenly reality the Holy Spirit wants you to see, like the spiritual beings inhabiting the Cosmic Temple with which this book is primarily concerned. The job of imagination is to span this whole gap between fantasy and eternal realities. So, how do we learn to walk this bridge effectively?

Step one: pray. Submit yourself to God, and do whatever you need to in order to feel connected to Christ's help and protection. Then, get on the bridge, even though you may not be sure which side you're on. The more time you spend on that bridge, the more experiences you'll have to compare, which will make the difference between fantasy and spiritual reality easier to discern. Even when you're completely sure that all you are doing is entertaining those flighty fantasies, stay on the bridge and keep trusting those impressions. Remember, you can always test the fruit of the experience when you're done. I'll give you a personal example of this issue that still makes me laugh today.

It was very early on in my practice of these things, and as I would normally do, I took some time in the morning to open the eyes of my heart and find Jesus. On this particular day, the first thing I imagined was Jesus as a train conductor standing alongside an old steam-engine train. My first thought was, "There's no way this train is real." But I stuck with the impressions and got on the train anyway.

To make a long story short, the train went up a mountain, into the Cosmos (sound like a flight of fancy yet?), and finally to a beautiful landscape. Jesus was still there with me, although no longer dressed as a train conductor, and as we walked into that perfect environment, I knew that we were somewhere important. I spent the rest of that morning walking around a manicured garden with Jesus, carrying on a conversation in real-time on another plane.

Looking back, I'm sure there wasn't *really* a steam-engine train in a spiritual dimension waiting to pick me up. I think that image was the best facsimile that my imagination could give me that day – to help me "get there," so to speak. The train, itself, I would call a flight of fancy; but notice in that story that the willingness to get on the train led to an experience that was far more substantial. As we went further, the flightiness gradually faded away, and I found myself firmly in that unseen, yet real, place.

In this case, the train was like the bridge we've been talking about. It was my way of walking from one function of imagination to the other. Had I discounted the whole experience based on the randomness and ridiculousness of the steam train, I never would have followed my senses to that morning's paradise.

And now, many years later, I can say that my time spent crossing the bridge has grown less and less. What I mean is it's far easier after years of experience to be on the heavenly side of imagination from the get-go. With years of systematic practice, I've gotten used to my mind's silliness, which makes that part easier to skip past. Conversely, the more time spent in that unseen, eternal realm creates a familiarity with those spiritual realities we all hunger for. It's the practice that makes you familiar with the whole bridge of imagination, and that gives you the freedom to choose on which side of it you'll spend your time.

When I teach about imagination, I normally keep it as simple as possible because most people just need some permission to give their imaginations a chance. But to do the subject justice, and to allow it to be as powerful as possible, we've needed to take a deeper dive. The bridge metaphor, along with the rest of this chapter, is there to show us that while imagination can be trusted, that doesn't mean it's always right. Or we could say that one side of imagination is the side we can trust. Those flights of fancy along the way should be discerned and discarded, especially if they aren't good. It's those "not good" parts of imagination that we need to discuss next.

| 26 |

Is Imagination Safe?

As this is our last chapter on imagination, I think a short recap is in order. We started with the idea of inspiration, that historical notion of Divine encounter, perception, and creativity. We tracked the evolution of our connection to those divine functions from inspiration to imagination, and we saw how this journey parallels the development of mankind. As we've been on this odyssey of self-discovery, matters of all kinds have become increasingly internalized. So, it stands to reason that a word like "imagination," which describes a distinctly internal process, would eventually describe how we connect to the unseen world from within ourselves – with a part of ourselves.

From there, we could see imagination in a new light, going far beyond our modern notion of fantasy and revealing itself as a powerful spiritual faculty that we can use to see spiritual things – if we so choose. The fact that we have to choose to use this faculty in a conscious act of will, not as an unforeseen moment of Divine blessing, also parallels the development of participation we've charted, since final participation is a conscious choice to participate with the spiritual presence in Nature. If all of this makes us think of maturity, as if God is trusting us with some personal responsibility, then I think that fits the narrative of mature sons being revealed who will one day free Creation.

And finally, since our use of imagination as a bridge to connect to that unseen world is initiated personally, it introduces concerns about how badly we could mess all of this up. That's more or less where we landed after the last chapter, with a realization that trusting imagination comes with some inherent risks, like the possibility that we could be led astray by our own imaginations. So if flights of fancy and the potential for evil imaginations are all present in the human condition, why on earth would God encourage us to use the eyes of our heart?

I'm reminded again of C.S. Lewis's Chronicles of Narnia series. In the story *The Lion, the Witch and the Wardrobe,* the children are discovering that Aslan – the Christ figure of the story – is, in fact, a big lion...

> "Who is Aslan?" asked Susan.
> "Aslan?" said Mr. Beaver, "Why don't you know? He's the King...
> "Is – is he a man?" asked Lucy.
> "Aslan a man!" said Mr. Beaver sternly. "Certainly not. I tell you he is the King of the wood and the son of the great Emperor-Beyond-the-Sea. Don't you know who is the King of Beasts? Aslan is a lion – the Lion, the great Lion."
> "Ooh!" said Susan. "I'd thought he was a man. Is he – quite safe? I shall feel rather nervous about meeting a lion."
> "That you will, dearie, and no mistake," said Mrs. Beaver, "if there's anyone who can appear before Aslan without their knees knocking, they're either braver than most or else just silly."
> "Then he isn't safe?" said Lucy.
> "Safe?" said Mr. Beaver. "Don't you hear what Mrs. Beaver tells you? Who said anything about safe? 'Course he isn't safe. But he's good. He's the King, I tell you."

I often come back to this passage when I need a reminder that very few things in life are risk-free, and this is especially true if a person desires to follow Christ. Eventually, if you are serious about growing closer to God and realizing God's image in you, you're going to have a moment (or many) that requires you to take a leap of faith without knowing the end results. It's just a part of following Jesus. That doesn't mean those leaps of faith and their inherent risks are bad, but rather, that we have to constantly lean on God's goodness. Safe? No way. Good? Absolutely, abundantly, yes!

Now apply that children's story to the use of imagination to see spiritual things. Is it completely safe? No way. We have our flights of fancy to contend with, and our own capabilities to conjure up evil things. We could even look to history to see that if we use our imaginations to perceive a spiritual voice in Nature, it's at least possible to invoke those fallen angels familiar to our pagan ancestors. And, what if we can't tell the difference between the fallen and the holy? There's a reason the Bible warns us to test the spirits. The potential for deception is there. Not mentioning it would be dishonest.

If you're thinking this is a reason to shy away from any trust in imagination, that's not the case. However, it is a reason to do all of this the right way, which is not on our own, but with a developed relationship with God. I wouldn't suggest anyone trust spiritual senses – of any kind – without a deep understanding and appreciation of the Holy Spirit dwelling inside us. If you've found this book by accident, this is the moment where you must consider your own acceptance of Jesus Christ as the King of kings that He is. With Him, things can be both risky *and* good. Without Him, trying to re-establish a connection with a spiritual presence in Nature on your own, you inherit all the risks without the protective covering of that Christ-lion in Lewis's story.

In short, doing this outside of a connection to Jesus is like playing Russian roulette. There's no guarantee it will bear good fruit, and an almost certainty that it would produce far more bad fruit than was ever necessary to experience. But if you are in Christ, you have an anchor for this journey, and that may be the only thing that qualifies a person to trust the eyes of their heart. It will be God's goodness to us that keeps our mistakes in check and our fantasies corrected so that our internal eyes focus on what is good and true and holy. Therefore, setting the intention of your heart to perceive *with* God, instead of just on your own, is at least one way to minimize the risks.

One way to do this is to make sure you're seeing Jesus with you constantly as you explore the unseen realm, almost like a chaperone for your experiences. Now, if you're new to all of this, you might find the idea of picturing Jesus in an imagination exercise a foreign idea. If that's you, you'll find some of my earlier books helpful. Again, to give the briefest of versions here, most people begin using these senses by imagining Jesus with them in their room, or in a peaceful, restful place like an imagined garden of Eden.

The whole idea is to let all of your senses work (imagination isn't just seeing, it can be hearing, smelling, etc.) so that you can be aware of your closeness to God.

What I found after years of doing this sort of thing, and I know I'm not alone, is that time spent with God in the Spirit opens a door of discovery to so many good, holy, heavenly things. Once our eyes are open, it seems God can't wait to show us "the riches of His glorious inheritance." Rediscovering the angelic nature of Nature is just one of those heavenly things He seemed intent on showing me, and I'll tell you some of those stories in just a moment. But first, let's get back to Jesus being a chaperone for our sometimes-fanciful imaginations.

Let's say I ask you to picture the garden of Eden, and your first impressions are of something hellish. Or what if I ask you to imagine sitting at a table with Jesus, but all you see is a shut door and a sign that says, "You're not wanted here."? And, God forbid, what if I ask you to imagine the spiritual presence in the thunderstorm, and what you get is a vengeful, lustful Baal or Zeus? All of these are examples of something "not good."

Some aren't good because they're not true, like the hypothetical situation I just mentioned where a sign tells you, "You're not wanted here." It would be an immediate red flag to me simply because it's not something Jesus would ever want. We can discern those things and discard them on the grounds that they don't line up with God's character as we've learned in the millennia of recorded Biblical history. But what about the things that aren't good, but are also real, like the presence of fallen angelic orders we've already established as historically accurate? It's not like they disappeared since the Scientific Revolution.

Keep in mind that we are talking about participating with a heavenly realm, and the Apostle Paul noted that there are spiritual forces of evil in those spiritual planes (*Ephesians 6:12).* It stands to reason that if you open the eyes meant to see into those places, eventually you are going to see something that opposes you. Simply put, you should expect to encounter some dark things, and given how much of our imperfect selves is involved in the process, we should expect this journey to also be imperfect. Enter into our experience that protective, powerful Christ-lion that Lewis wrote about.

Let's take each of my hypothetical bad scenarios in turn, but with a conscious eye turned towards our heavenly chaperone, Jesus. If I were imagining the garden of Eden, but only saw a dark, dismal, foreboding place, I would immediately ask where Jesus was in this picture. Then, I might say something like, "Do You see what I'm seeing?"

If my impression is that He says, "Yes," then I know I'm going to follow up with, "Then what are we doing here?" I would spend the rest of that imagination moment sticking as close to Him as possible and waiting to see what He intends to do to bring His light into such a dark place.

If I felt rejected when I was trying to meet with Jesus around His table, I would do the same thing. I'd imagine Him there with me and tell Him, "I know that I keep seeing this sign that says I'm not welcome here with You, but I know that isn't from You. That's not who You are. So, who put it here, and what should we do about it?" Once again, leaning on God's goodness and allowing Him to chaperone would reshape that moment. Perhaps He would reveal it as a flight of fancy to be discarded, or maybe even a lie from some fallen spirit that needed to be dealt with. In either case, that might lead us to a healing moment with Him.

Lastly, if I encountered a spiritual being that was not *for* me, or wouldn't acknowledge the preeminence of Christ, or behaved in any way that contradicted the fruit of the Spirit, I would again make sure

Jesus was present. From there, Jesus can lead the way in moving past that adversary, and if He so chooses, into a different introduction with a spiritual being that is for me and not against me.

Each one of these scenarios has happened to me personally, in one form or another, and it has always been a focus on Jesus, the Christ, that made sense of the experience, or corrected it, or dealt with its demonic origin. There's just no way to overstate the importance of doing this *with* God and allowing God's character to be the standard by which all imaginative experiences are assessed.

While this book is not a "how-to" guide on using your imagination to connect to spiritual realities, I felt it necessary to include this section for two main reasons: we need to know how powerful our imaginations can be if we're going to re-see the spiritual beings in Creation. And we need to know how to do this in a way that doesn't return us to the paganism of original participation.

The sprinkle of imagination theory and discernment guidelines are in here to keep us on that narrow path. Additionally, and this is just my gut feeling, the job of freeing Creation will be done by folks whose imaginations have developed even further than our current practices. If I've successfully made the case that imagination acts as a bridge between the world as it is and the world restored, then further development – and deeper understanding – seems like a given.

Now before I move on to telling my own stories of angels, Nature, and restoration, I'd like to give a few last words of advice for anyone who wants to attempt the same sort of thing. First, you're going to get stuff wrong. Don't let that discourage you. Keep trusting those first impressions and test the fruit as you go. If it doesn't line up with God's character, discard it and try again. Once again, never underestimate the blessing of Jesus as the imagination chaperone.

Also, it's very likely that by using the eyes of your heart you'll find areas in your life that need healing. Don't ignore it. Invite Jesus in and let Him speak to those issues. If you process the things that go wrong *with* the Lord, it's likely to increase the fruitfulness of this whole endeavor, not to mention the rest of your life.

Lastly, know this: every story I'm about to tell you was accomplished using the imagination. For me, it was never an out-of-body experience or any other kind of transcendental state. It was all done using the simple gift we call imagination. The process was incredibly natural. The results were incredibly supernatural. Whether you call it imagination or the eyes of your heart, using it is the first move we can all make to allow the Cosmic Temple to be a temple once more.

Part 3

Stories of Freedom

| 27 |

Believing in Angels

I had a little chuckle to myself when I outlined the structure of this book. I imagined saying to you, the reader, "I wrote everything in those first two sections to give myself total impunity to say the things I'm about to say!" No, really, just between you and me, the issues of natural history, science, and imagination are there to make these stories not sound so outlandish. In truth, they are. They are stories from another world really, and hopefully the first two sections of this book have at least set the stage for why this sort of thing is not only real, but a necessary part of our human development. Without any further preamble, I think it's best to start back at the beginning and tell you how I came to believe in angels in the first place.

It was my first year of using the eyes of my heart to see the heavenly plane. I was used to spending hours with Jesus, just hanging out with Him in the garden of Eden, or following Him into whatever part of that universal, New Jerusalem He felt I needed to see. Visits to God's throne rooms and my never-ending questions about what was happening were both commonplace. On one day in particular, and as usual without me knowing to ask for it, I met an angel. He stood in front of a gate that led into the heavenly Jerusalem, and as we approached him, he took a knee and made his introduction.

I can only think of one other time before this when an angel told me their name, and when that happened it didn't feel like that big of a deal. But when I asked this angel's name, and he offered it, I knew something was different. The name I've come to call him, after all these years, is *Brennadan*, or just Brendan for short. It means "prince."

I had a feeling when we met at that gate that this angel and I would be close, and from that day on he was a constant presence joining me and my Savior as we traversed the heavens. He was my angelic ally. My first, and longest, angelic friend. And in case you're wondering, no, none of this was easy to understand at the beginning. As a Christian, we're taught that Christ is the center of everything, and to let nothing vie for that central place reserved for the Messiah. This is a good thing! It should never change, no matter what happens in our imaginative sight. But, when Jesus introduces you to one of *His* friends, you have to at least expand your circle of interest to keep up. I kept checking in with Jesus to make sure my focus was in the right place, and He kept affirming me, but it took a little more convincing from another heavenly figure before I could understand what Jesus was up to.

To tell that story, I'll have to refer back to a passage about angels from my previous book, *In the Palaces of Heaven.* I spoke about Daniel and his major leap forward in angelic understanding, but I left out one important detail. That entire teaching came from Daniel, himself. You read that right, Daniel (from the Bible) visited me for a time as I opened the eyes of my heart to instruct me on how man's relationship with the angelic world has changed over the years. I didn't mention it when writing that earlier book because I thought it would be one other-worldly claim too far for the reader. Well, the cat's out of the bag now, and this is as good a moment as any to say this: if you're going to look into the place to where Jesus ascended, then you're just as likely to see all those saints seated with Christ in the heavens as you are likely to see an angel. Daniel is alive and well in Christ, so if you hang around Jesus *where He is currently enthroned,* who knows what good things you'll encounter? For now, let me just summarize what Daniel taught me about the angels...

Before Daniel, mankind never knew the proper names of the angels. Or at least they were never written, which, as we've seen in other parts of human development, is important. Daniel, at any rate, is the first person in Biblical history to record their proper names. He's the first person to acknowledge that they can be called a proper name like Gabriel or Michael. That's almost 3,500 years of recorded Biblical history without one angelic name. It's important to note here that there were plenty of names for the fallen angels masquerading as pagan gods. But this was the first moment God opens the door the way it was intended.

In my meetings with Daniel, he went on to show me that after his own watershed moment with Gabriel and Michael, other angelic proper names came in, whether it was in the apocryphal writings or in the book of Enoch. It is from those sources the names Uriel and Raphael have been passed down. He went on to point out Gabriel's further involvement in the Gospels and Michael's involvement in Revelation, along with all the other angelic activities recorded in that book. The point Daniel was making was that man's relationship with the holy angels was strengthening. It was like a great cosmic crescendo from those early days of introduction to the frenzied activity at the close of the Biblical canon.

But the crescendo didn't stop there. It carried on in the tradition of the desert fathers and eventually took another giant leap in early Celtic Christianity. St. Patrick, that first Irish apostle, met with an angel named Victoricus, or Victor for short. Read any early account of Patrick's life and you'll come across this angelic helper. But more than that, in at least one annal of his life, it is said that Patrick met with Victor like a friend. In the thousand or so years since Daniel, angels had gone from the nameless forces of Nature to other-worldly friends.

Daniel wanted me to see the big-picture trend. He wanted me to see how God had been bringing humans ever closer to the angelic world, and that the quality of relationship was increasing. It would be some years before I fully grasped how important this could be, but at least now Daniel will get the credit he deserves. It's just amazingly unpredictable what you'll find when you open your imagination to Jesus.

You might wonder why this trend of closer relationships with angels is not discussed in church. It's not an unjustified omission, as I think we all have some healthy fear about meeting angels. On the most basic level, I think it feels a bit beyond our control, since we're interacting with something from the other side of that spiritual veil. That's the "other-worldly" part of it. But then there's the deep-seated genetic memory in humanity that remembers what went wrong in Eden. We listened to an angel – a spiritual being – who did not have our best interests at heart. It left us with the notion that "angel" could equal "deceiver." Well, Daniel certainly proved that wasn't always the case, and his history lesson gave me the confidence I needed to continue my own angelic crescendo, so long as the fruit remained good and the centrality of Christ was ever-present.

| 28 |

Introductions

In those early days, many of my moments "in the Spirit" were on a ship, sailing through the heavens. I could barely contain my joy as I felt the cosmic wind fill the sails, and it truly felt like I was doing something I was created to do. Brennadan would often be with me on the ship, his bright purple raiment and silvery crown identifying him even when my spiritual eyes could just barely take it all in. He was an excellent guide. It seemed he always knew the path we should take, and he always had the keys to open up any doors. I came to think of him in those days as the Navigator, and his power to guide and my desire to keep sailing seemed the perfect match.

Stop and think about all of this from Jesus' perspective. According to the Gospel accounts, the Messiah was aware of the angels around Him, a fact that can only be reinforced by His current position, sitting enthroned in the heavens. These angels are not distant strangers to Him either. According to the Scriptures, they (and all things) were made by Him and for Him. These beings are lovingly and wonderfully made, and as I hope we've established by now, they are known personally. So, imagine how happy it must make our Lord when He gets to introduce us – His friends – to these wonderful spiritual beings He's created! This is exactly the way it felt to me as Brennadan and I got to know each other, but my angelic introductions were far from over.

Acting the part of the guide, Brennadan was there to introduce me to other beings, and I still think, to this day, that he was introducing me to an angelic family. They all seemed to be connected, as if they functioned as much like a tribe as did the people of ancient Israel. And each one he introduced me to created new categories for angels that I had never previously considered. At the start (and we'll get to how it changed in a moment), Brennadan looked very human. I think this is the sort of thing that would lead Daniel to say of Gabriel, "then, the *man*, Gabriel..." But Brennadan didn't look completely human. He had a heavenly appearance, so to speak, as if he were made of different, more luminous stuff, and his garments and crown always seemed of a design that could pass as either ancient or futuristic all the same. I think his appearance, heavenly yet relatable, was the perfect introduction, and it helped pave the way for angelic appearances that challenged my understanding.

I met an angel who seemed to be made of fire, his skin and hair plasmatic. There was an angel who rose out of the ocean, blue-skinned and watery. His crown was ornately finned on either side, and he carried a spear made of lighting. The first feminine angel I met seemed connected to the earth. Her garment was a rich green and she was constantly surrounded by animals and growing things. I met angels armored from head to toe, and then some who were made up of glowing, gold light. One of those light angels turned out to be Uriel, the first archangel I ever met. His garments sparkled like a diamond, and his hair was made of pure white light. He was so bright that I could barely discern a face. Fitting, since his name means, "God is my light."

If (since) this all made Jesus happy, then it made me even happier still. This brand-new world had opened to me, and without realizing it, I was already categorizing the angels. That's a human thing to do and shouldn't be diminished. I think we inherited that role from our first estate, when we named the living creatures, so applying it to the angelic realm seems natural. Our minds are meant to connect the dots in our world, and the predominant connection in these first angelic introductions was that I was perceiving them as a part of Nature. They each seemed *made of* a part of creation, including the ones that defied immediate associations. For instance, that fully armored angel turned out to be a Virtue, a specific type of angel personifying those untouchable parts of creation like Love, Generosity, and in my case, Patience.

If I needed any more proof of the angel/Nature connection, I got it in the form of another spirit-being I came to know well, whom I called, Marshall. He looked like a thunderstorm condensed into a human form. His garment was all blues and greys. His crown was embedded with lightning bolts. And he told me he would fight for me when I needed it. In many ways, it was like meeting a holy version of that fallen spiritual being, Thor, who was immortalized in Norse myths. We got along great, and as I've chronicled in another book, he's really helped me out a few times, none more impressive than when he intervened in a wedding ceremony.

The basic story is worth repeating here, and it's a story I often tell simply because it was one of the first moments that the connection between these spiritual beings, Nature, and the effects it can have in my mortal life all came together. It took a friend's wedding, which I had the honor of officiating, to set the stage. It was an outdoor wedding, and when the ceremony was due to start, the thunderstorms moved in. The sky worsened, a few raindrops began to fall, and as the wind gusted, the groom had to steady the canopy under which he and his bride-to-be were standing. In that moment, sensing a doomed wedding ceremony, I opened the eyes of my heart and spoke to Marshall, who personified the storm.

He agreed to help, and the clouds parted. The wedding was beautiful, and not a minute after the guests were dismissed for the reception, the clouds opened up. The rain came down in torrents, and as I was scrambling to pick up a few things, the wind finally blew over the canopy and the pole cracked me on the head. I looked up to find a smiling (or was he laughing?) Marshall who seemed to enjoy the prank. My getting hit on the head was his way of saying, "See, you needed the hour for that wedding, and I gave you exactly an hour." In truth, it was the punctuation I needed to realize how much the storm and I were really connected.

I mentioned earlier that this thunderstorm angel reminded me of an original, holy version of Thor (albeit more elemental in appearance), but the connection between the angels I met and the old myths was increasing across the board. It's a common occurrence that the more you use the eyes of your heart, the better you perceive. Or we could say that with practice, your imagination is refined. The way that you first see an angel is rarely the way they look years later, provided you keep looking. In this case, with continued experience, most of the spiritual beings I knew well took on a more mythological appearance, which led to the moment I finally found out who my friend, Brennadan, really was.

From time to time, I had seen him with a white eagle for a companion, and occasionally with wings on his crown. When he showed up one day with winged sandals and holding a set of scales, the similarities to a certain mythological figure were hard to ignore. I'm hoping our history of Nature and science sections have instilled in you an appreciation for mythological history, as a kind of history that includes unseen elements that were just as real in our experience. And if you've looked into that part of human memory, you might have come across an image of Hermes, or Mercury, who bore that winged attire. A much harder-to-find historical reference from ancient Greek pottery (it will come as no surprise that I stumbled upon it accidentally) reveals Hermes even holding a set of scales. Once I put together the appearance of this angel with the job I always saw him doing, it all made sense. Hermes was a spiritual being that personified travel and the transitions from the mortal to heavenly world, among other things, which seemed to match my angelic friend's specialty in heavenly navigation.

For the first time, I could see him as Hermes or Mercury should have been – the original version rather than the fallen god counterfeit. This was the spiritual being that God created to personify those specific parts of the Cosmic Temple (travel, crossroads, commerce, etc.) who never fell. It was also the first moment I was struck with the obvious – if there are kinds of angels like Hermes/Mercury that fell, and there are many angels that didn't fall and remained in their Godly order, then there must be other Hermes-like angels that have remained in their holy positions this entire time! I've made the point earlier that there must be many spiritual beings that personify each part of Creation, and it's a commonly held Christian belief (based on some passages in Revelation) that Satan only took one-third of the angels with him in his rebellion. Therefore, there must be a holy Hermes (probably many), and Brennadan was this *kind* of spiritual being. From that day on, in my own spiritual perceptions, he has been like a holy, restored Mercury.

Brennadan typically ushers in "the firsts" in my imaginative journey, so it's not a surprise he gave me my first glimpse of a restored, spiritual Nature. I had just never considered, before that moment, that something like the planet Mercury, which I've seen at twilight close to a setting sun, could be restored to me. What I mean is, Mercury has only ever been a god of mythology or an inanimate planet. What I never thought was that it could be both an object in the sky *and* a holy spiritual being, present with me all the time in my internal senses. It was as if a part of Creation came to life and began speaking to me again. It felt like the first, tiniest step into final participation, that promised future mentioned in Romans, chapter 8.

I came to love all the planets in exactly the same way, and I found some of the angels I had already met were just waiting for me to connect the dots. Many of them were also both mythological beings and restored astronomical planets.

I'm not sure if everyone will find the same things I did when they open their imaginations to the Cosmic Temple, Jesus the Christ, and all His holy angels. Perhaps for some, it's not the planets that speak to them, but the stars, and for others, the Virtues. Maybe the birds of the air, or the trees, and the spiritual beings that inhabit those parts of Creation will reach out to you when you open your eyes. It's entirely possible that those parts that reach out for relationship with us are the very parts of Nature we have been personally commissioned to set free.

| 29 |

Overcoming Fear

The mythological Hermes (or Mercury, I'll use them interchangeably) was a spiritual being who could cross over from the heavens to the earth, and even under the earth. The ease with which he crossed those barriers was one of his hallmark traits. Participating with Brennadan, as a holy version of this kind of angel, was like getting to know a part of the kingdom of God called *crossing over*. Or maybe we could call it *transitions*. That is at least one part, if not a preeminent part, of what Brennadan personifies. And it is no surprise to me that those issues have taken a center stage in my life. My interest in grand cosmic transitions, called ages, and the simple journeys into the heavenly realm through imagination has been greatly influenced by the time spent with the spirit of those issues.

I've made it a priority to keep our heavenly access simple and accessible to all. These things are so often presented as the activities of "elite" Christians and off-limits to everyone else. I was never in that elite, super-spiritual category, and so I wanted it to be known that this phenomenon of experiencing heaven was possible for anyone in any walk of life. I've taught many to open the eyes of their heart, and I've tried to lay out practices so that it is easily replicated. And, I've had the privilege of taking many groups of people "in the Spirit" so that we can learn to exist in that realm together. I want to give credit where it's due here: I attribute a big part of the success of these practices and the expansion of the knowledge of participating with the heavens to an actual and functional relationship with Brennadan, the one who crosses over. To be sure, I'm not taking Christ out of this equation at all, but simply giving appreciation to a part of Creation that was made by and for Christ.

You might be wondering, "How close are you two?" The answer is an interesting story, and it's the most important revelation that has come out of knowing my angelic friend, at least to date. But to set it up, let me go back to that other part of Nature I've come to know – the storm. You might get the impression from my previous description, that the angel in the storm I called, Marshall, has a powerful presence. You'd be correct. I would sometimes see him so large and powerful that his size and scope looked a lot like the towering thunderclouds I've come to know living in the southeastern United States. On one occasion, while taking an afternoon walk, I noticed him standing among a brewing thunderstorm.

In this case, I was using both sets of eyes at the same time, superimposing what I could see in the Spirit with what my biological eyes perceived. So I was looking at the tall thunderstorms and the giant presence of Marshall at the same time. He looked massive and powerful. I thought to myself, "If my ancestors could perceive this, then I know why they mistook him for a god." And that's when I started to worry. Was I getting off track and thinking too highly of these angelic persons? Was I close to committing the spiritual crime of worshipping another god?

With a sincerely worried heart, I backed out of my spiritual perceptions and just went about my walk, but within a few minutes from home, Marshall came to meet me again. He must have known I was on shaky ground, because he appeared to me much smaller. A side effect of practicing the use of the senses is an increased sensitivity to what is going on in that world across the veil. This was one such case, as this second meeting was prompted by him, and I simply responded to the nudge. I'm glad I did, because what he said next answered a lot of questions for me.

He began with, "Christopher, have you ever been to the Grand Canyon?"

"Yes," I replied.

"And were you in awe of the Grand Canyon with its size and majesty?"

"Yes," I said again, "it was an unforgettable sight!"

"Did you worship it?" Marshall asked.

"No."

He continued, "And when your friends do nice things for you and help you, are you thankful?"

"Yes," I replied again, seeing where this was going.

"And did you worship them?"

"No," I said.

"So, awe and thanksgiving must not be the definitions of worship." And with that last comment, he left to take up his perch among the towering cumulonimbus clouds.

I've thought a lot about that moment, and it went a long way to ease my mind about how awesome and mighty these spiritual beings could appear. It freed me up to let them be true personifications of Creation itself, without taking anything away from the majesty of God. It also changed my understanding of true worship, as I now think of it as any activity that acknowledges in whose image I was made. As I mentioned before, we see things better and more accurately the longer we look. This is just one more example of that, and it was necessary to see Marshall as he really is without fear. If that fear would have been allowed to persist, I doubt I would have continued to grow closer in relationship to him, and that brings me back to my fateful meeting with Brennadan, and yet another moment when I had to face some fears.

| 30 |

Believing to Befriending

A few chapters ago, we recounted the journey from knowing angels by their proper names (thanks, Daniel) to the friendship enjoyed between St. Patrick and Victoricus. I'm not sure what this would have been like for Patrick, but a few years into knowing Brennadan, I would have sworn we were well on our way to some kind of angelic friendship. However, my angelic navigator knew otherwise, and he brought it up one day as I was sitting on my office floor, using the eyes of my heart to see into the heavens.

You should know that, by this time, I had become very comfortable with his presence. We talked every week, sometimes every day, and the subjects we covered in conversation were both vast and cosmic. As I'm sure you've gathered, I'm inquisitive, and Brennadan (whether he liked it or not) ended up receiving many of my questions. I mean, how could anyone wander about the heavens and not ask, "How in the world is this even happening!" The running joke about me in the heavens is that for every question I've had answered, I have 20 more. Jesus is the one who first said that to me through a teasing, loving grin. The picture I'm trying to paint for you here is that I frequently asked questions, and talking with Brennadan was like having a well of wisdom at my fingertips. The "doors" he could open, as a holy Mercury, and the thresholds he could cross, were not just in space and time, they were also doors of the mind and of ideas.

On this particular day, as I set cross-legged on the floor of my office, I could also perceive him there with me, and I was just about to ask another question. That's when he said to me, "Christopher, I don't want to be just a heavenly encyclopedia for you. I don't want our relationship to consist of you coming to me when you have a question, picking me up like a book and rifling through my pages until you find the answer you're looking for."

I was stunned and sorry. I immediately apologized because I knew what he said was true. I hadn't meant for that pattern to evolve like that, but it did. It wasn't that surprising either. I was just learning about the Scientific Revolution and our changing relationship to Creation when this conversation took place, so I wasn't shocked to learn that I saw Brennadan, as a part of Creation, as a tool to be used, not as a personality to know. I am a product of the modern scientific world, after all. My default setting is to exploit the resources around me.

What came next was an even greater shock. Since I was genuinely contrite, I asked Brennadan what he wanted, since I knew it was wrong to continue as we were. To this he simply said, "All I want is you."

Maybe you read that with a tender voice, and that was certainly the manner in which he said it. But that day, what I heard triggered a deep fear. It seemed like a spiritual being from beyond the veil was asking for a quality of relationship with me that I reserved only for the Godhead. There was only one Creator, one Lord, one God, that I would *give* myself to, which to me meant giving my trust, adoration, love, and vulnerability. I think this is true of anyone who cultivates a close communion with God. It's a sense of being fully given.

When Brennadan said that he just wanted *me*, my mind went to the same place of concern as when I saw Marshall's power and immensity in the thunderstorm. I felt that if I said "yes" to this, I would be giving Brennadan that special kind of trust I only gave Jesus, and that would constitute some sort of false worship or idolatry. At least it would feel like they were on the same plane or hierarchy in my mind. Now,

I'm sure you can guess that this situation turned out to be a beautiful lesson, but it's important for you to know the misgivings I had that made this moment all the more necessary. And I think there are a few more disclaimers worth giving before I tell you the rest of the story.

Some of you might be reading this and wondering why I processed this the way I did. You might be saying, "Christopher, Brennadan wasn't asking to be in God's place in your life, he was just saying that he wanted to be with you as you are, not in a constant question mode." If that's you, thanks for taking up for my righteous, true Mercury; and you're not wrong. In hindsight, it's easy to see that his statement was caring and benign. But heaven knows us well, and God knew this conversation would take me somewhere good. Additionally, I had come to trust Brennadan greatly. He was, and is, unwavering in his love and devotion to God. He's always pointed towards Jesus, the Christ, never away from Him. Nevertheless, what I heard that day caused me to question how I was using my imaginative senses and where they were taking me.

Secondly, you might be saying that I worry too much. You might even ask, "If the fruit of all of this had been good, why the deep concerns at every turn?" The answer is simple. I'm aware of the possibility of distraction and deception. I'm also aware there might be good reasons humans don't attempt these kinds of things out in the open. Perhaps it's all too easy to get off track. My own defense, which I've already mentioned, is to stay very focused on the person of Jesus, the character of God recorded in Scripture, and the fruit of the Holy Spirit. Testing what we encounter through imagination should be taught as a non-negotiable part of seeing the unseen. If doing that makes us slower to process, or makes us walk more circumspectly, we are the better for it. In short, never feel bad about going slow, taking the time to test the fruit, and bringing everything before God, which is exactly what I did about this situation.

Okay, not immediately. When Brennadan said that he just wanted me, I took a long, imaginative look at my friend and politely told him that I was not sure that was something I could give. Then, I closed my spiritual eyes and for a few weeks never reopened them as I processed what had happened. Again, if you put yourself in my shoes, you might feel as I did the concern of crossing a line that shouldn't be crossed. I thought to myself, "If you get this close to an angel, will it be good and holy, or a repeat of the deception recorded in Genesis?" After a few weeks, and no closer to a conclusion, I set my heart on opening my internal eyes again, and this time I was greeted by a presence that exuded trust and compassion. It was Father God, waiting for me to "come up here" and talk again.

The Father greeted me warmly and walked with me to a large, old oak tree, set on a grassy plain overlooking the ocean. The whole environment was peaceful and just what I needed, as was the Father's large, jolly, and protective presence. Some folks ask me how I perceive the Father. The answer is that I've seen Him many different ways, from a mind-blowing Creator swirling with power, to a familiar, fatherly presence, dressed in simple robes of rich colors and smiling the kind of smile that makes all fears disappear. Both appearances make me feel wonderfully small and young. This meeting was with that familiar, fatherly presence, and He wrapped one of His massive arms around me as we walked over to the tree where He sat me down. It was there with my back to the tree, looking at Him with His back to the blue ocean, that He began this conversation.

"So, Christopher, I've heard that Brennadan asked for more of a relationship with you, that he just didn't want to be used as a tool in your toolbelt but wanted a real relationship."

"Yes, that's right, and I wasn't sure that's something I should give him. Won't that infringe on the specialness of my relationship with You?"

"Christopher, I'm going to tell you more of My story."

At this point I was close to another freak-out moment. The last thing I needed was more revelatory information. What I wanted was a few Scriptures and a hymn to settle me down, not some extra-Biblical story, if that's what was coming. Furthermore, I was well aware of other religions that liked to tell stories of how "God came to be God."

I wanted nothing to do with those sects and I made all this plain to the Father. He smiled and continued anyway.

"Christopher, when I created the angels, I gave them power to affect My life." He let that sink in a moment and then continued,

"You've read that thousands upon thousands attend to Me [from the book of Daniel]; if their attendance didn't have power to move Me, then what good would it be? What meaning would it have if their ministrations didn't change My position or state? It would all be a cruel joke if their ministry to Me was without power to actually do anything, wouldn't it? It would be as if I lived in some ivory tower, so high above everything else that nothing could ever touch Me."

Then, in a comical way, the Father added,

"Could you imagine Me and you in that ivory tower, high above anyone's touch, and me telling you, 'I had to find something for all these angels to do, so I told them they could attend to Me, but just between the two of us, I'm so high above them that nothing they do ever affects Me. But, don't tell them that. I just had to come up with something to get them out of my hair'."

That would be a cruel joke indeed, I thought.

"No," the Father went on, "I created them with the power to move Me. Let Me show you how that began..."

"To create them, I took power and life from within Myself, and I poured that power out so that they could exist. I took the light from within Me, and I poured it out and created all the spiritual beings that personify light. I took the waters from within Myself and created all the angels that give voice to the waters. I did the same with the virtues, the winds, wisdom, glory, the land, and everything else that exists in Creation."

"When I gave away that power so that they could live, I never took it back. Their existence was a gift, and that power was theirs to use. My covenant with them was this: I'm giving you power to affect My life; what you do with it is entirely up to you."

"And when they stood there, encircling Me and realizing their life and power came from Me, they exclaimed, 'This One had all of the power and gave it away so that we would exist! Surely, this is the Most High!' Then, with total adoration for what I had given them and created them to be, they reached back to me with that power they had been given, attending to Me with it, lifting Me up, and glorifying Me – affecting My life."

The picture that the Father gave me was that of a completed circuit or the flow of a magnetic field. The power had gone out from Him so that they would exist as the embodiment of Creation, and when they attended to Him, they poured that power back to God, just like the way a magnetic field arcs from the north pole before flowing back into the south pole.

"But," the Father said, "it didn't stay that way forever. One angel in particular, the firstborn, the personification of light, questioned his motive for attending to Me. He began to think to himself, 'Wait a minute. This One had all of the power and gave it away? This One gave this power to us? Why, if we stop attending to Him, won't He be powerless?'

"It didn't stop there," the Father said, "soon, the questions turned more arrogant, and that light-filled spiritual being began to ask, 'What if I'm the Most High? What if I'm the one with the most power? I was made before the others and given the greatest glory. Perhaps I should be at the center of this circle?'

"And with those questions, the angel simply removed his hand of attendance and stopped his own power from returning its flow to the Godhead. His neglect turned to frustration. His frustration grew towards animosity and finally rebellion and war. By that point, he brandished his disgust with Me to the other spirits, 'What are all you fools doing? Don't you see that He had the power, and then gave it away to us? He's nothing if we stop attending to Him! We will go to a place where we can be the power and never again bother to attend to Him!'

"And so they left. They descended from My presence, which was the source of their nature and existence, and away from Me the purity of what they were started to degenerate. The separation from Me allowed their pure forms to pervert into something wrong and corrupted. They became the vice to every virtue for which they were created. But I was never going to leave them there, and I was never going to dissolve my covenant with them. I had given them power to affect My Life, and I wouldn't take it from them. So, I met them where they were, in the form of a mortal human. I came to them through Jesus of Nazareth, who was God in the flesh."

I'll tell you here, dear Reader, that at this point I was seeing this story as much as I was hearing it. In my mortal body, I was sitting on the floor of my office in what anyone would assume was a prayerful state. In the Spirit, I was sitting with my back to the oak tree, watching the Father tell this tale with the blue ocean behind Him. And as He was narrating this part of history, I could see it all happening like I was watching a movie. This was especially true once we got to this part of the story, when God's covenant was put to the test in the person of Jesus, the Son of God...

"Through Jesus, I had every opportunity to break my covenant with the fallen angels. I could have simply wiped them away as they stood between Me and My purpose. In fact, in the garden of Gethsemane, when the soldiers came to arrest My Son, it's said there were legions of angels at His disposal to stop the forthcoming brutality, but I had made my choice from the beginning that they could affect My life with their power, and I was not going to break My part of the deal. So, they arrested My Son and eventually crucified Him, but it is written in 2 Corinthians that if the rulers of this age had known the mystery of God, they would not have crucified the Lord of glory.

(My thoughts here: whether you think of "rulers of this age" as the human ones or the fallen angels, either way, the former was being directed by the latter)

The Father continued with this cosmic look into Jesus' last week, leading up to His death...

"The fallen angels had been waiting for a moment to reach out to Me and affect My life again. They had become perverted and deranged from what they once were, and they were sure that when they affected My life this time, either they would dispose of Me forever, or I would relent and break My original covenant with them, which would have the same result. It would make Me a liar."

"So, during that week leading up to the cross, those spirit beings came to My Son and attended to Him with what they had become. The angels that once personified the virtues of Kindness and Gentleness had perverted themselves into the personifications of Violence and Brutality, and they struck Him through the fists of the soldiers beating Him. The angels that personified the beauty of green, growing things like the leaves of a laurel crown, had fallen and become the thorns of a fallen world, and they attended to Him when the crown of thorns was placed on His head. The spirits that once embodied Blessing had descended to become curses, and attended to Him with what they had become as people came by to curse and spit on Him as He hung on the cross."

"All of them came back to complete the circuit in those final days, reaching out to Jesus to affect His life just like they did with Me in the beginning, before their fall. And as My Son hung there on the cross, itself a perverted form of a tree, all the fallen spirits waiting in the wings came to lay their hands on Him, completing a covenantal circuit established from their creation. They poured into Him what they had become, and His heart burst."

(My thoughts here: many people have looked into the death of Jesus, and a common conclusion is that He did not die by asphyxiation from crucifixion, but rather by some cataclysmic cardiac event. Some say that His heart literally burst.)

The Father continued, "The last fallen one to touch Him that day was once an angel of Life, Health, and Healing, not unlike Raphael, but had now become the personification of Death. And Death reached to Him, attended to Him, and dragged Him down into the grave. But, Christopher, they didn't understand the mystery of God, or they would not have been so bold as to attend to Me again, as they were doing with the person of Jesus. When they reached for Him, they were acting according to our original covenant. They had power to move Him, but when they completed that arcing circuit, they poured back into Jesus everything that they had become. They thought it would be the end of the story. Instead, all that they were became Mine and His. All their power became the Lord's. They inadvertently gave back the power over everything they had become. This is why it is written:

> *I am the first and the last, and the living one. I was dead, and see, I am alive forever and ever; and I have the keys of Death and of Hades.*
>
> *– Revelation 1: 18*

"Christopher, through Jesus, a part of the Godhead came out of the grave holding the keys to Death and Hades because of this original covenant. It's the way I created them. I gave them power to affect My life; what they did with it was up to them. When Christ arose, it wasn't just as the Lord of all things good, but the Lord *over all things*, good and bad. His name was the name above every other name. With this one act, I affirmed my Lordship over all of Creation, both the perfect original and the fallen counterfeit."

As I listened to this account of the death and resurrection of Jesus, told from the unseen world, I was aware that my mortal body was crying. But there was still more story to tell.

"Christopher," the Father said, "Brennadan asked you for a real, true relationship that day. Real relationships take vulnerability. If you're in a place where the other party can't reach you, or affect you, you're trying to be invulnerable, and that one-way street is not really a relationship at all. Think of the friendships you've attempted where this was the case, either with you or the other person. Aren't you aware, eventually, that one person is willing to be vulnerable, but the other person is not? Isn't it obvious when you share your life with someone, but they don't share theirs in return?"

"Yes," I replied, starting to see the reason for this whole conversation.

"And think of a marriage relationship, which at least should be the most vulnerable one you experience. Even in the wedding vows themselves, isn't vulnerability written in? Think of the vows that give that spouse power to affect your life, 'in sickness and in health.' Ultimately, vulnerability is giving power away, and it's the nature of any meaningful relationship. You choose to let down your walls, which gives the other person the chance to reach you. Move you. Affect you."

"So, what Brennadan was asking for was a true friendship. He was asking for something mutually vulnerable. When he said that all he wanted was you, he was giving you his most heartfelt desire. He just wants to know you and relate to you even if there was nothing you could ever gain from each other. That would be a real relationship. The kind where you choose to relate simply because of a love and appreciation for each other, without a thought of how it can be used."

I looked up at the Father from my seat against the oak tree and said, "I think I need to go have a talk with Brennadan, since I'm pretty sure I've been afraid to be vulnerable with the angels You've introduced me to. But I have no idea what to do next."

The Father smiled His wonderful smile at me and said, "If your Father gave away power to the angels so that they could affect His life, what do you think you're going to do?"

| 31 |

When You See Me

There are moments in everyone's journey with God that are too rich to unpack in just one sitting. Some things are supposed to be pondered over time. This was one of those moments for me, as it decisively changed what I thought about relating to angels. If you remember from the beginning of that conversation, the problem was that I wasn't sure I was supposed to be vulnerable with these blessed angelic friends. I didn't think I was supposed to "let them in," so to speak, into my life. The Lord was the only being, in that heavenly plane, to whom I gave that privilege. What the Father was teaching me, however, was that I could resist that all I wanted, but a real relationship required vulnerability, also called "giving power away." The entire introduction to our talk was there to show me that God didn't create things that He keeps at a distance. He doesn't know the angels by an impersonal number. He knows them by their *name*.

God's love and nearness to Creation should one day be reflected in us, the image and reflection of God. Since we are God's mirror image, I would expect everything that God has said or done to one day be reflected back to the Godhead through the only part of Creation designed to be that perfect reflection. And when it comes to giving power away, just consider the actions of Jesus, Himself. Watch how He constantly gives power away as He walks this earth. We mentioned this in our chapters about the meaning of true human kingship. Jesus is never consolidating power to Himself. He has never desired to live in the proverbial ivory tower, so far above His subjects that they could never reach Him or move Him.

Personally, I believe that the moment God feels that start to happen, He gives more power away so that the entire Godhead is always touchable and reachable. God wants to be with us. God wants to be with the Creation. You have to give power away to be relatable. Just think of Jesus' ministry and you'll see that as His own power and influence grows, He finds ever larger groups of people into whom to pour His power. First the 12, then the 70, and through the Holy Spirit given by His actions, that power has spread throughout all humanity. There is no denying it: we are made in the image of a relational God, who would rather die than be distant from us.

I think this one moment with Brennadan was invaluable, as it showed me once and for all the kind of kingdom I've joined. It showed me that if I'm to be a reflection of my Father, then one day I would take up that same mantle, to know those around me and this wonderful Creation with the same capacity for love and vulnerability. If I'm like Him, then one day I'll know what it means to give power away. And perhaps, this lesson with Brennadan was there because it was time for me to start learning the connection between freeing Creation and mutual vulnerability. Wouldn't that be amazing, if what creation really needed this whole time was a mature son who could be to it as the Godhead is – loving and capable of a real relationship?

I set out to practice this very thing. Keep in mind that I thought about it a lot. This was not something I jumped into haphazardly, and I would never suggest to anyone that their next step should be to find the angels closest to them and blurt out, "I'm here to give you power to affect my life!" There's just too much that could go wrong without some really good foundations in place. And, no, that's not a return to spiritual elitism, given how I despise that. What's needed here is focus, not fear. We need to focus on what's good and holy, all of which can be found in the person of Jesus. And when the Cosmic Temple does introduce itself, in whatever forms you have a calling to hear, take some time to build the relationship naturally. Let Jesus continue to be the chaperone and allow the relationship to become more meaningful. Isn't that the way it's supposed to work? Don't meaningful relationships take time?

With Brennadan, there was a history of relationship we'd already shared. This moment was simply the push to go from believing in his existence to becoming a true friend. I'm still feeling the push, and I sincerely wish I were better at all this. I often get frustrated with my unbelieving heart and my modern, distracted lifestyle. One day that frustration boiled over as I was perceiving Brennadan with me in the Spirit. I saw him approaching me and I just couldn't bear to see him. I felt like I was doing a terrible job relating to him, and I felt the need to say sorry again for being so dense.

I began with, "Half the time I forget that you're here, and the other 45% of the time I treat you like a tool to be used. There's maybe 5% of the time that I actually relate to you as a friend. Did you get in trouble with God and I'm your punishment? Did you lose a bet with another angel? Did you draw the short straw? Really, why do you put up with me?"

He smiled at me and said, "You have no idea what we get out of this do you?"

"No," I replied, "I'm pretty sure this must be torture for you." In truth, Brennadan never seemed put out by how long it takes me to adopt something new. He was always reminding me that it was a giant leap forward to be talking like we were, and there was no need to feel bad. Nevertheless, I was in this moment, and I was not prepared for what he said next.

"Christopher, when you look at me, I exist."

I stopped what I was doing. I looked at him and what dawned on me either on my own or with his help (not sure it matters at this point) was a new appreciation of what it means to be made in God's image. If you recall way back in the chapters on the Cosmic Temple, the word image is "idol." It's as if we are all representations of God's person, formed out of the clay, and displaying in our diversity the myriad aspects of God's Persona. But at our core, we are of the same *kind* as the Godhead. We were made in that reflection. Consequently, the core of who God is would be in us as well, albeit spread out in all those being conformed to that image.

So what is at that core? This is just my opinion here, so feel free to take it with a grain of salt, but once the Godhead had poured out all of that power to give life to Creation, there are only a few things left that God could not, or would not, give away. Namely, the essence of God's Being. The waters, the skies, the stars, Love, and Wisdom were all created by God pouring those things out of God's self so that they could exist on their own. What was left at that center of God, after everything in those first six days of creation had been poured out, was existence itself.

Consider the name of God "I am that which I am." Or more accurately, "I will be that which I will be." Isn't God's name a description of existence? Certainly, God is love and wisdom and all those good things. I've been contending that God gave all those things a life of their own, if for no other reason than to give power away and remain relatable. But what I'm suggesting here is that God, and all those made in God's image, are formed as the nodes of reality itself. In other words, to be made in God's image is to be the end point of reality and existence, with God being the starting point, of course. So what might Brennadan have meant that day?

He went on to say, "Christopher, when you acknowledge me, you're bringing me into this world of incarnation. You (all humanity in general), are what makes things real." Think on this for a moment. It would not be surprising at all that for things to exist, they must be connected to God, or the images of God. It would be no wonder then that even the fallen angels seem to be bound to humanity and need our agreements to make their plans reality. As an aside, it is not lost on me that there is a metaphysical interpretation of quantum mechanics (largely rejected) that claims this very thing – human consciousness is what creates reality.

For now, perhaps we can see this as yet one more affirmation. If we find any of this to be true (the metaphysical approach to quantum mechanics or the essence of God as the Person who embodies existence itself), then we might find even more reason to reach out to the spiritual beings standing at the ready to be *brought into* Creation once more. Those revealed sons mentioned in Romans, chapter 8, are revealed precisely because of their resemblance to the One in whose image they were made.

| 32 |

Hades, Wealth, and Generosity

I'm often asked the question, "Does all of this time spent getting to know the angels take away from your time with Jesus?" It's a good question, and I'm always glad someone asks it because it reveals a heart that wants to stay close to the truth. For a myriad of reasons, I've felt even closer to Jesus through it all, as what this journey has revealed about Him and how much He trusts us draws me ever closer in. But it's also the simple practice of following His lead. This whole time, I've been going where He wanted me to go, and meeting whom He wanted me to meet. I've kept checking in with Him through each new development, just to make sure I'm still doing okay, and He keeps prodding me along as I get to know His world.

The issue here is that we all have limited time, and we're wary to take any of our limited focus off of Jesus and onto something that seems peripheral. There are two solutions to this. First, make more time. I don't say that in jest, but it's a fact that looking at things unseen requires you to take the time to look. At the end of the day, I think we'll find we can handle some peripheral issues if we just cut out a little meaningless drivel here and there. Second, if you're taking on this kind of journey and you feel it taking you away from Jesus, stop what you're doing and just focus the eyes of your heart on Him. He can lead you to reconnect with Creation in a way that keeps the first things first. Just keep in mind that following Him is never dull, especially when He's ready for you to meet another part of the Cosmic Temple.

And it was just such a moment that led to another cosmic odyssey. Jesus came to me in one of my imaginal times and reflected with me on how I had met the spiritual beings that personify the planets. All but one, that is. I had never met Pluto, which seemed like a good exception since Pluto was synonymous with Hades, the mythic god of the dead and the underworld.

Jesus asked me, "Why have you never met Pluto?"

I felt like the answer was obvious. "Because that would be the personification of the underworld and the dead! Why would I want to meet a fallen part of the Cosmic Temple?"

"I see," Jesus said. "But are you able to find beauty underneath your feet?"

"Yes," I replied. "There are gemstones and crystal caverns and who knows what else that we've not discovered."

"Right, and wherever you can find beauty, I'm there. Furthermore, the old mythological god of the underworld was also the god of wealth, and isn't that ultimately something good? Aren't Wealth, Value, and Prosperity Godly virtues?

Now Jesus had my attention. It's true that all of the things humanity has ever used to represent value have come from under our feet. The gold standard, which was the standard for all monetary value until the last century, was based on the gold we mined from below. And all other objects we've used to embody wealth and riches have come in the form of diamonds, rubies, sapphires, emeralds, etc., which are all found underground. It's no wonder our ancestors associated the underworld with wealth. Even in our modern world, we're still looking underground for the riches of oil and natural gas. And the most modern form of money to date, cryptocurrency, is said to be *mined* in a hardly understood process involving computer servers, often buried underground.

I must admit, I imagined the underworld as the Devil's domain, filled with fire and brimstone, demons and darkness, and of course, the grave itself. Looking back, I think a lot of those ideas are more influenced by Dante's *Divine Comedy*, that medieval narrative poem that described the descending layers of hell below us. Or maybe it's a carryover from myth, as if the old god, Hades, was just another name for Satan, and they are both somehow the spirit of Death. No matter the cause, I had never considered that a spiritual underworld could be good. Or at least that a part of it could be good.

Jesus continued, "I want you to go meet the holy version of Hades, the real personification of wealth and the underworld. It's not all the Devil's domain down there. It's a realm I created, and it has both beauty and purpose."

And just like that, the Lord was leading me to open my heart to another part of the Cosmic Temple. I accepted the mission and set off on another spiritual adventure, looking for the holy or *true* Hades, although I doubted that would be his name when I found him. There's even some name etymology for Pluto that provides the meaning "giver of wealth," but I doubted he would be called that either. But if there was a fallen spirit that embodied wealth and the underworld, there must also be one who never fell and upholds the truth.

As I would often do when Jesus sent me off on some errand, I sailed to the underworld on my ship that can traverse the heavenly planes. If you're looking for an explanation here about how one can sail to the underworld, think of it as a journey into a spiritual plane, not unlike a journey to the heavens. But in this case, it was like going to an *underneath* heavens, or *underheavens.* Since I had never dreamed of an undertaking like this before, I made sure to take some courageous angels with me that I thought could help if we encountered anything nasty (we did).

Cosmic geography aside, one of the first stops on my underworld odyssey was a giant cave filled with treasure. Like many medieval stories, that treasure was guarded by a great dragon. However, this is where the similarities to the old dragon stories ended, as I never made any attempt to slay him or take the treasure. I simply asked his name, which he said was Greed. Obviously, he was not the one I was looking for. We left him there and continued on to a place that looked a lot more like my "Dante's *Inferno*" view of the underworld – a vast cavern and a lake of lava. Set right in the center of the lava lake was a black pyramid. At the top rested the nasty presence I alluded to above, a fallen spirit personifying the evil force of Isolation. I'm giving this detail here, as the order in which I found these fallen ones makes for a great metaphor. Isolation came after Greed, which could be interpreted this way: Isolation is the end result of Greed.

Our journey continued on a bright, electric blue, underworld river, which led to another meeting with a spirit that personified the system of money, and possibly financial systems of every kind. While he didn't appear nasty, he wasn't holy either, and so the search continued as I spent time in my internal/spiritual senses. Finally, in a vast underworld cavern, so large it could have held entire city blocks, there sat an old, worn-down castle. It looked to be in ruins as if from centuries of neglect. Instinctually, I knew I had found the place, so my companions and I started exploring this old palace, slowly making our way to the center.

There we found a central courtyard with an ancient well. Sitting on the edge of that well, on the crumbling stones, was the angelic being I had been sent to find. As we entered, he looked up and said, "I have been waiting for someone to come down here and find me."

Every day I was there, I watched his palace come to life more and more. Water began flowing in all directions from his palace and out into the vast subterranean cavern. The walls of his home, once drab and neglected, were filled with all kinds of precious jewels. And out past his underworld domain, I sensed an entire forest made of silver trees with gold leaves. It was beautiful, just like Jesus had insinuated from the beginning. Those days I spent with him in his angelic home were like watching a part of Creation come back to life. Or maybe it was a first taste of freedom.

This holy Hades and I got to know each other in my time there. He told me about the former greatness of his home, which was slowly being restored with each day I was there. He talked of seven rivers that flowed out of his great house, bringing the different forms of true wealth to the world of mankind. He taught me about each of them, and the first ones he listed were things like friends, children, education, and story. For this reason, whenever someone shares with me their story, I feel like they are heaping treasure into my life.

He spoke of his counterpart, a feminine spirit-being named Generosity, who personified those rivers that once flowed up from his abode. She was nowhere to be found, but those rivers were flowing with ever greater intensity with each passing day. I'll comment here about the notion of angelic gender and companionship. Once again, history can inform us, as every ancient culture assigned a gender to the angels (or spiritual beings) with whom we related. And it was not uncommon, especially in myth, for these beings to be paired with a consort of the opposite gender. Since Nature, as well as myth, is expressed in the pairing of opposite genders (even opposite charges of electricity), it seems completely natural to me that we would find this in every spiritual plane we can perceive.

The stories he told of his wealth and her generosity working together was the stuff of restored myth, and as I felt my time there coming to a close, this holy Pluto had a few more things to share. He spoke to me about human memory and how all that has *passed away* naturally goes to a place under our feet. It's our *past* that we bury in the ground, which is why archaeologists must dig things up to know how things were. In this respect, the human memory was just another one of the treasures hidden in his storehouses.

The embodiment of wealth had something to say about Jesus, too, and that's a recurring experience with each of the angelic beings I've come to know well. At some point, they share an insight about the Christ that magnifies God and, frankly, encourages me that I'm on the right track. In this case, he wanted to tell me about Christ's death and resurrection. He reminded me that according to the Scriptures and our Christian creeds, Jesus died, was buried, and descended into the grave. And He was there until the third day. When He arose, He did so with a resurrected body, which must have been different in some manner because everyone had a problem recognizing Him, not to mention the completely miraculous things Jesus did in this resurrected body before He ascended.

That much I knew, but what the spirit-being of wealth wanted me to consider was that the only place Jesus was for those three days was the underworld – the grave. The only place He could have put on His resurrected form was in the one part of the Cosmos where treasure, wealth, and value are kept. There He put on a body more valuable, more expensive, and more adorned than the one that was crucified. He was wearing it when He came out of the grave. And, like gold, it was incorruptible. If you didn't know this, one of the things that makes gold so special is that it doesn't decay. It's one of the things most impervious to the effects of entropy. Maybe that's why it's been a standard of value all these years.

On one of my last days there, the restored Pluto and I walked among the gold-leafed silver trees surrounding his palace, and there he gave me a name I could call him. It sounded like *Adamah Noel*. Word and name meanings bring out the nerd in me, so I always do a little research when an angel gives me a name. A simple translation of his name would be *Earth-born*. It fit nicely.

The day came when my companions and I got back on the ship and sailed out of the underworld. As we traversed that electric blue river, another ship passed us, heading back to the newly restored palace. Standing at the bow of the ship was a beautiful feminine being, with long, dark hair and a flowing blue gown. It was Generosity, herself, coming back to her home with Adamah Noel.

This whole adventure is a picture of what I think intentional participation will look like. At least in the beginning. I'm sure the kind of meeting I just described is only the tip of the iceberg when it comes to restoring and freeing the Creation, but it's a start. Nonetheless, it changed me. I will never look at the underworld the same again, and I'll always keep in mind that what we've only known as the grave is much more like a treasurehold of wealth and memory. Or maybe it's even the dressing room of resurrection, as that might be the place we put on our incorruptible body. After all, the resurrection of the dead originates from beneath our feet, in a place that's personified by a spirit I've come to call a friend.

> *For the Lord Himself will descend from heaven with a shout, with the voice of the archangel and with the trumpet of God, and the dead in Christ will rise first.*
>
> *– 1 Thessalonians 4: 16 NASB*

Not long after this underworld odyssey, I found my connection to Adamah Noel filtering into my mortal life. As it happened, I was away speaking at a conference, and at the end of a meeting, someone felt led to finance my next book project. It was a hefty cost, and I wasn't quite sure how the funding would work, but it was all taken care of with one check – one piece of wealth placed in my hands. What I found out when I got home was that while that check was being placed into my hands, my family met someone in need at the grocery store. Without any questions, they had agreed to help a single mother get back on her feet. Almost simultaneously, and while we were separated by hundreds of miles, my family was participating with both Generosity and Wealth. I'm not claiming one preceded the other by rule, simply that they occurred together, as we've come to know them. That was the first of many encounters with these complementary parts of the Cosmic Temple.

| 33 |

Freedom

I've selected these stories because I think they best illustrate what it's like to get to know a spiritual presence in the Cosmic Temple, but also because they tell of what can happen when we move from exploitation to relationship. Remember, this isn't about us being in control of Creation or the other way around. It's about finding a mutual appreciation and honor that reflects the love and care our Lord has for what's been made. It's hard to cherish something that you're exploiting. Conversely, it's very hard to exploit something you truly cherish. But when we get the relational part right, we should expect to see good fruit. It should change things for the better, both in our lives and those around us.

I also think these stories illuminate what it's like to find the original, holy design of what has only lived in our minds as fallen, mythic spirits. It was certainly a revelation for me that the Mercury or Pluto our ancestors knew was derived from (fell from) a holy archetype that is still there to be discovered today. And so it happened that on my way out of the underworld, I came across yet another spiritual being waiting to be reimagined. Although with this particular being, C.S. Lewis might have beaten me to it.

I took my time sailing back home after meeting Adamah Noel. Now that the underworld wasn't just a dark and foreboding place, I found myself lingering in underworld caverns filled with giant, luminescent crystals. Otherworldly plants and hidden waterfalls filled my internal senses, and the exoticness of it all was as heavenly as anything else I'd perceived to date. And in this hidden world I met another spiritual presence, clad in green garments, reddish hair, and a jovial smile. He was wild, in the way I sometimes imagine Jesus appearing untamed in contrast to our religious sensibilities. Around him swirled the life of this exotic world, fairy-like beings, tigers, lynx, and what I would best describe as the kind of creatures you'd read about in The Chronicles of Narnia. There were fauns and nymphs, even centaurs, drawn out by his presence. And everywhere he went, there was growth. Vines and plants sprouted and grew, bringing lushness wherever he went.

If I had seen these kinds of things early on in my heavenly journeys, I'm not sure I would have continued on. I'm sure I would have assumed I was out of line or that my imagination had taken me too far in the wrong direction, but by this point I was at least willing to pursue the unusual. Meeting a holy Hades at Jesus' direction will do that to you. And this angel's presence was reminding me of something I had read about before, like how Brennadan had reminded me of Mercury.

Our ancestors knew of a being that personified wine, merry-making, and weddings, and was accompanied by exotic animals like leopards and tigers. He was called Bacchus, or Dionysus, and all his wine and merry-making was believed to personify freedom, a fact seen in his alias, *the Liberator.* In some myths, he's even involved in the dead coming back to life. But as with all things pagan, it was at best a mix of good and bad, and at worst an utter moral disaster. And so, with Bacchus, he wasn't just the wine, he was drunkenness. He wasn't liberation into true freedom, he was a license for excess and orgiastic degeneration. "Bacchanalian" is not a positive adjective. Now, put your empowered spiritual perceptions to work – if this is a fallen being, what did he fall from? What is the original, true, and holy presence that stands today as what the pagan Bacchus should have been?

Since the historical Bacchus is the counterfeit of true freedom, I wondered as I beheld this lively being if he could be the true form, the

"Bacchus," if you will, that never fell. That brings us back to C.S. Lewis, who I think was also interested in imagining a holy kind of Bacchus. Before we get into Lewis's imagination, let's first remind ourselves that Jesus was familiar with angels, and they attended to Him as He fulfilled His earthly ministry. We have the Gospel account of angels ministering to Him after His 40 days in the wilderness, and Jesus mentions He could call on a legion of angels if needed. But what happens when we open our eyes to the angelic presence in all Creation? Might we see more interaction between Jesus and the angelic world?

When C.S. Lewis took a crack at how Jesus might co-labor with the angelic realm, he did so with Aslan, that great lion who represents Jesus in The Chronicles of Narnia, and none other than the spirit-being Bacchus. It occurs in the fourth book of the series, *Prince Caspian,* and the two are seen together as Aslan comes back to Narnia to wake up the world from its slumber. If you're familiar with the book, you might recall that Narnia was full of life and talking animals. Yet, through a process that looks a lot like a Narnian scientific revolution, the world had become mute and lifeless. It had lost its spiritual essence.

That's when Aslan comes back, and he brings with him the mythological Bacchus complete with his wildness, grape vines, and celebratory processions. He's accompanied by the forest fauns and nymphs and together they restore – or free – Narnia from its slumber. It's a powerful scene, and one might gawk at Lewis's choice of such a scandalous character as a friend of Aslan. Perhaps Lewis's choice was based on more than a flight of fancy.

Jesus' ministry began at a wedding. Of all places and events, He chose a wedding celebration as the moment to reveal Himself. He performed His first miracle there when He converted water into delicious wine. He goes on from there to bring freedom to those in pain, sickness, and oppression. He raises a widow's son from the dead, and who can forget the moment He calls Lazarus from the grave? When it came time to enter into Jerusalem, He does so in a procession of singing, dancing, and rejoicing. All these are Bacchus-like themes. Additionally, we can see a very Bacchus-like metaphor at work when Jesus speaks of the vine and the branches. Is it any wonder that C.S. Lewis paired Jesus (Aslan) with this type of spiritual being?

We are not saying, of course, that Jesus was partnering with the pagan Bacchus. And we aren't claiming that a Bacchus-like angel was responsible for Jesus' ministry, either. What Lewis expertly uncovered was that at least one of the angelic presences chosen to accompany Jesus had to have been a holy (or original) Bacchus-kind of angel. It is the holy Bacchus parts of the Cosmic Temple with which Jesus participates throughout His ministry – one could argue more than any other part, except perhaps healing. And why wouldn't He? He is the Lord over all, and *Freedom, Wine, Merry-making,* and *Resurrection* are all parts of the Creation that were made by Him and through Him. The fact that a handful of Cosmic spirit beings, each personifying things that were essential to His ministry, kept close to Him shouldn't surprise us at all. After all, there are archangels and cherubim doing this very same job as they surround God's presence in the heavens. We would expect this set-up to be mirrored in the person of Jesus, since He is the fullness of God in bodily form.

Once Nature comes alive, and virtues like *Freedom* are given a voice, then it's easy to see far more angelic interaction in Jesus' life. Add to this the significance of that historical, pagan Bacchus to our ancestors, and we might get an even clearer picture of why Jesus chose him as one of His essential angelic helpers. Bacchus was one of the oldest spiritual presences known to the ancient Mediterranean world. He was one of the first presences sensed in that early, instinctual participation. One reason for that could be that this part of the Cosmic Temple, even in its fallen form, is foundational to life. If that's the case, it would provide yet another reason why a holy Bacchus served the King of kings as they went about restoring the foundations of humanity.

Predictably, God had a plan in introducing me to another angel I would one day call "friend," and as you can guess, I didn't call him Bacchus, even though I suspected he was the same (albeit holy) kind of angel. I knew him by the name Arden, which I learned later means "great forest" (a quick Google search of name meanings can sometimes affirm our spiritual perceptions). I thought the picture of a great forest, filled with life and growing things, fit him well. He was the personification of those things that I was meant to find – the wild liberator given to me as I live out my own calling on this earth.

Part of that calling was played out in my few years as a high school teacher. I taught both science and philosophy, the latter just to seniors, and on many days, Arden was my supernatural assistant. Before the students would arrive, I would watch him dance into my room, his procession of mythic creatures and beings following his tune. The vines would grow about the walls, bursting with grapes in an unseen world overlapping my earthly classroom. And above all, the virtue he embodies, Freedom, saturated the atmosphere until it permeated what would otherwise have been a mundane lesson. For when I was aware of our connection – our participation with one another – my students would ask the most profound questions. Loosed by an unseen freedom, they would wonder aloud at the majesty of Jesus, or the message of the gospel, or if there is still a supernatural element to life. I had the privilege of watching many of them discover for themselves that God was good, loving, powerful, and capable of doing wonders.

It wasn't just grapes that grew on Arden's vines. Thoughts, ideas, and revelations burst forth as another part of the Cosmic Temple took a step towards freedom.

> *Now the Lord is the Spirit, and where the Spirit of the Lord is, there is freedom.*
>
> *– 2 Corinthians 3: 17*

| 34 |

Blood and Healing

I never could have predicted that Arden would help me become a better teacher, or that Brennadan would reveal what true friendship was all about. I had no idea that the thunderstorm could teach me about true worship, or that the underworld could redefine my notion of wealth, but it makes sense that a released Creation would have a lot to offer the images of God. Also, I think it's fitting that the first fruits are internal changes, the kind that push us towards a full expression of Christ. And as what's inside us grows, it's inevitable that we see the fruit outside of us in Nature as we've come to know it.

I've chronicled just a few stories here of interactions with both inner and outer Nature. Changes in myself and changes in my environment. They're both important, and my hunch is that the outer changes will increase with each passing year. I mentioned in the introduction that I've by no means achieved some harmony with Nature that when I step outside the birds come rest on my shoulder and carry on a conversation. But I have seen glimpses of what that might be like, and it's not simply metaphoric when the Scriptures hint at the same:

But ask the animals, and they will teach you;
the birds of the air, and they will tell you;
ask the plants of the earth, and they will teach you;

and the fish of the sea will declare to you.
Who among all these does not know
that the hand of the Lord has done this?

–Job 12: 7-9

It reminds me of a time I was bedridden with a back injury. I'd spent a week or so unable to stay upright for more than a few hours, and in all honesty, I was having a pity party as I lay there wondering when I would get my life back. It was springtime, and from my bed I could see our backyard and what was turning out to be a beautiful day. While I lay there feeling sorry for myself, a bluebird came right to the window and began to sing with all his might. My ears heard notes, but my spirit heard the words, "Get up, Christopher! Go for a walk! It's a beautiful day; you can do it!"

I argued back to him, "You don't understand, every time I get up it hurts."

"Don't lie down anymore," he said, "Get up and go for a walk anyway!"

I agreed. I laugh as I write this that I actually argued with a bluebird, but his song was just what my spirit needed. I got out of bed, took a walk, and never went back to lie down. The birds of the air told me that day how to be healed, and I believe that bluebird genuinely cared that one of God's kids was in need. I wonder if I cared as much for him?

There are other stories to tell of glimpses of a restored Nature, whether it's more encounters with the weather, or the times when a friendship with Time altered the course of events in supernatural ways. They're all beautiful to me, and there's no need to tell all of them, as the goal of this book (and perhaps even the transition to the next age) is for you to have your own encounters. Towards that end, I've selected one more adventure that I think encapsulates the results of using the eyes of your heart, systematically, for years. It illustrates how it changes us, focuses us on eternal, unseen things, and allows the Cosmic Temple to function with all the life with which it was created.

There was a family we knew that was in the midst of a terrible trial. Their young daughter had been diagnosed with leukemia and had been fighting the disease for almost a year. We had prayed for them, but I'll confess this situation was on the periphery for me, and many days had gone by without my thinking about this family or their sick daughter. Then came the day when a text message was forwarded to me with a request for prayer. The situation had turned a bit desperate, and the mother had sent out a plea for prayer support as her daughter was struggling mightily. She had received a bone marrow transplant, but her body wasn't responding well. She was very weak, slept most of the time, was dealing with infections from the various ports placed in her body for medicine, and couldn't eat. The treatment's effects on her digestive tract made it too painful to swallow anything solid.

And so, the forwarded text came to anyone who might pray, for now was the time for action. Although I had not been close to the family or this situation, as soon as I read the text I knew I must do something. I immediately opened the eyes of my heart and saw myself in the Spirit. I'll note here that after years of doing this, I'd grown accustomed to seeing myself completely restored, with a resurrected body that I think my closest friends and family would find unrecognizable. It's the "me" that Christ will raise from the dead, incorruptible and fully in His image. On this particular day, I saw myself dressed for war, and I prepared to find out what dark spiritual force was hindering this girl's healing.

With my spiritual senses ready, I did another thing made possible by years of practice: I imagined the girl's hospital room, and I went there in the Spirit. I perceived myself bursting into that room, fully armored and ready to fight, and the first thing I sensed as I scanned the room was the risen Lord, Jesus, standing at the foot of the girl's bed.

What followed was a humorous moment as Jesus took in my battle-ready state and, with a wink and a smile, said, "Simmer down, Christopher, we've got it under control."

"Well, it looks like I got dressed up for nothing," I responded. He then called me over to where He stood, looking lovingly at this child He knew so well. He mentioned that her blood was not balanced, due to the transplant, and He called Blood into the room. Blood is a created thing, and as part of the Cosmic Temple it has an angelic spirit that personifies and embodies its essence. And so a beautiful, crimson-robed being glided into the room. I watched this holy angel stretch out both hands to the girl as she lay asleep on the bed, and blood flowed into her in what can only be called a cosmic transfusion.

My only job was to observe, and while I stood there next to the King, He said to me, "Do you remember where you've been traveling to in the heavens lately?"

"Yes," I replied. It was common for me to be sent around the heavenly realms in my journeys in the Spirit. You'll recall I'm friends with a heavenly navigator, so running errands for my Lord is commonplace. As it happened, I had just been to a small cottage placed in a large field of tall grasses and wildflowers. Horses of different colors grazed there, and while I found it beautiful to visit, I hadn't discerned any other reason for my journey to that little corner of paradise.

"I want you to take her to that meadow with the horses," Jesus said. At His leading, the three of us left that hospital room and headed to the meadow. When she arrived, she immediately went to play with the horses, and after some time, Jesus took her into the cottage where the Father and Holy Spirit had set a table for her that was filled with food. The girl sat down to eat, while Jesus and I stood at the door. I was looking for some explanation as to what was happening at this moment, and if this was Jesus' way of taking her home eternally. He smiled at me and said, "Christopher, I'm going to be here with her while she recovers. All the time she's sleeping, she'll be here with Me, eating at My table and playing with the horses in the meadow."

I left her there in the presence of the Trinity and sensed that my assignment was done. That same day, I relayed this experience to the mother, thinking it might be an encouragement. As it turns out, this little girl loved horses, and on the day she was diagnosed, she had just finished her first horseback riding lesson. But what surprised her mother (and me) was that the poster they used to decorate her hospital room during those long weeks of treatment was none other than a picture of three horses standing in a meadow of wildflowers! That was this girl's idea of paradise, and that's exactly where she was meeting with Jesus in her unconscious moments.

Within a day or two, her condition improved. Within a week she was able to eat. After a few weeks more, she was sent home cancer-free. It was a wonderful story to witness. The Lord was fighting for her. A part of the Cosmic Temple – Blood itself – ministered to her. Both Healing and the Author of Healing were present. And Jesus had prepared a place for her to recover, to which I had the privilege of navigating. The Cosmic Temple and the One who made it were on full display.

| 35 |

One Step at a Time

A common problem for anyone attempting to reimagine Nature is the mental gymnastics it sometimes requires to allow spiritual beings back into our worldview. Once you do attempt it, you might wonder just how much they're there, or on what scale. For instance, I think it's easier to imagine a mountain, ocean, or forest having a spiritual presence, but what about each individual rock, wave, or tree? In other words, how much of our reimagining is supposed to play out on a macro scale (big things) and how much on a micro scale (small things)? It's a tricky question, isn't it, because once you start drawing a line between what is alive with spirit and what is just an inanimate object, we're back on the road to dispiriting the Cosmos.

This is where I think it helps to review the cosmic geography of our ancestors and bring it forward along with our modern understandings. It will require some nuance, but it will probably help those mental gymnastics. As mentioned before, we can't unlearn what the last few hundred years have taught us, and we shouldn't want to. We can't unsee the world as objectified reality, with all its mechanisms and laws going on seemingly without any non-material origin. We can never go back to seeing a part of Nature, like the sun, as only the body of a spiritual presence.

What we need is a way to see the sun as both object and spirit, without causing our minds to buckle under these new demands. Let's think of the sun (and any other phenomenon of Nature) as a midpoint. On one side is man, and on the other is that spiritual plane. Set between them are all the aspects of the Cosmos we've come to know. Seen this way, the sun can be an object formed from natural processes, but it can also be the place where mankind and a sun-like angel meet. In other words, the object doesn't need to have a one-to-one relationship with a spiritual being, but rather serves as an appearance for all the sun-like angels God has created. The one we will sense in that object might be specific just to us, or perhaps it's a being that the entire region might know. You'll recall that different cultures sensed different personalities in the sun, so this sort of thing has been happening already.

In this model, what you see when you look at the sun (not literally, of course, you'll go blind) is not *a* spiritual being, but rather the meeting place for mankind and the whole host of angels God designed to represent the sun. In the same way, a forest is the *kind* or part of Nature where forest-like spiritual beings would interact with Man. Each part of the Cosmic Temple provides the space – the home – for the various kinds of spirit beings.

In this model, it wouldn't matter if we were thinking (or participating with) a single tree or an entire forest, a single electron, or a shaft of lightning, it is simply the appearance of a kind of angel, and that spirit is free to personify the part *or* the whole. If you need another metaphor to get the idea, you could think of the human body. I have hair, skin, eyes, etc., but it is all a part of who I am. And yet, my DNA can be found in all of it. So, perhaps you look out at an ocean and perceive one being whose form is made up of blue depths, shallow coral seas, and lapping waves altogether. Or perhaps you see a host of water-bearing angels, with each wave assigned to a particular personality, and each level of the ocean under the jurisdiction of a separate spirit. Both are perfectly fine options, and as we all learn to see the Cosmos holistically, I suspect two people standing right next to each other will sense different things. That should be okay for us, both because reconnecting to the Cosmic Temple is a highly individual process, and because we're new to this. The last thing we need is to become religious, or scientific, with the miracle of a blind man learning to see again or an amnesiac remembering who he is.

One bit of parting advice. Take your time. Each of us is uniquely designed to free some aspect of Creation. There's only One who can claim to free it all, and I'm just glad He's the Captain of our faith. For the rest of us, let's focus on what we love, because we'll always have authority in what we love. For me, I tend to look from the clouds up to the stars, and from the rocks down to what lies underneath. The stuff in the middle is often lost on me. My wife, on the other hand, excels with the flora and fauna all around us. On at least one occasion, I invoked her name when trying to connect with those parts of Nature. It was in the act of saving a bee, which we cherish as pollinators for our garden. The poor fellow was trapped in our screened-in porch, and he just would not let me get him out, despite how much I tried to convince him I meant him no harm. I finally broke down and exclaimed, "Just pretend I'm Melissa for 15 seconds!" He calmed right down, and I scooped him up and freed him. Sometimes it helps to know someone who knows.

As you begin to let your spiritual senses stretch out to include this wonderful Creation all around us, remember that it is all according to a design, and I sincerely hope you know the Designer. Furthermore, none of this is happening because the finished work of Jesus is somehow not enough. Knowing Christ is all any of us really need, and all the parts of Creation, whether it be light, virtues, wealth, winds, or fires, can be found in the One through whom everything was made. So try not to think of this as a solution to a problem God couldn't solve otherwise, but rather as an invitation from Jesus to enter into His world and experience the angels and Nature the way He does. That's what this really is, an invitation into His world. Lastly, think of it as a way to grow up into more of our birthright as God's sons and daughters, whose maturity just happens to be the thing that sets Creation free.

Notes

www.ingramcontent.com/pod-product-compliance
Ingram Content Group UK Ltd.
Pitfield, Milton Keynes, MK11 3LW, UK
UKHW041639190726
13854UKWH00006B/2578

9 798218 064358